ESG MATTERS:

How to Save the Planet, Empower People, and Outperform the Competition

DR. DEBRA L. BROWN
AND
DAVID A. H. BROWN

ESG MATTERS:

How to Save the Planet, Empower People, and Outperform the Competition

DR. DEBRA L. BROWN
AND
DAVID A.H. BROWN

ethos
collective

Printed in the United States of America

Published by Ethos Collective™
PO Box 43, Powell, OH 43065
www.ethoscollective.vip

LCCN: 2021912671

Paperback ISBN: 978-1-63680-047-9
Hardcover ISBN: 978-1-63680-048-6
e-book ISBN: 978-1-63680-049-3

Available in paperback, hardcover, and e-book

Any Internet addresses (websites, blogs, etc.) and telephone numbers printed in this book are offered as a resource. They are not intended in any way to be or imply an endorsement by Ethos Collective™, nor does Ethos Collective™ vouch for the content of these sites and numbers for the life of this book.

Some names and identifying details have been changed to protect the privacy of individuals.

"Every board member, regardless of the size of company, needs to read this clear and compelling explanation of why ESG matters and what they can and must do about it."

—Peter Dey, Chairman, Paradigm Capital, Corporate Director, Co-Author, *360 Degree Governance: Where Are The Directors in a World in Crisis*

"*ESG Matters* illustrates just how easy it is for us to do well by doing good!"

—Craig Larson, CEO and Chairman of the Board, Starion Bank

"ESG is an irreversible and powerful movement in capitalism and corporate governance, reflecting the fundamental importance of stakeholders - not just shareholders - both as a legal and a moral duty. This book is both timely and practical."

—Brita Chell, FCPA, FCA, ICD.D, Chair, Winnipeg Airports Authority

"Debra and David Brown have written a must-read primer for any organization wanting to know what ESG is about. I greatly appreciate their experience and wisdom."

—Rev. John Pellowe, MBA, Dmin, Chief Executive Officer, Canadian Centre for Christian Charities

"ESG Matters is the essential guide to understanding ethically and socially responsible strategy and governance issues. Stakeholders are now demanding that firms and organizations understand and engage with ESG strategies and measures. This comprehensive work by Brown & Brown is a thoughtful introduction and guide to encompassing ESG in organizations. I particularly appreciated the valuable ESG Pulse Check tool and helpful diagnostic questions that will help organizations get started on their ESG strategy and governance journey."

—The Rev. Dr. Marc Jerry, President,
Luther College Regina

"All good Boards need to include ESG in their agenda and ingrain it in the organization's strategic plan. From our climate crisis (forest fires and air quality), commitment on carbon neutrality to human rights challenges, ESG Matters will help you make this journey."

—Bill Chan
Board Director, Chair of the Audit Committee
Vancity Credit Union and Former
Senior Vice President and CFO
Encorp Pacific/ Return-It

To Larry Fink!
Thank you for your letters.

With special thanks to our editor, Lorna Stuber, Alex Martin our illustrator, and those on the Governance Solutions Team who made this book possible: Vicki Dickson, Rob DeRooy, Rafael Mazotine, Dave McComiskey, and Jake Skinner

CONTENTS

INTRODUCTION

Do you want to make more money, save the planet, empower people, have a clear path to your social license to operate, and outperform your competition? Did you know that Environmental, Social, and Corporate Governance (ESG) is the key to achieving those goals? In fact, organizations that adopt ESG standards are more conscientious, less risky, and more likely to be successful over the long term.

Saltwater Brewery, a Florida-based craft brewer, acquired three and one-half billion global impressions in a matter of days with zero dollars of media investment. Why and how did they reach such a milestone? Their success was because of ESG. The brewery cared about what its stakeholders cared about—the environment. Rather than spending their limited marketing funds advertising to their customers, many of whom are surfers, they created biodegradable and edible six-pack rings for their beer. No more worrying about plastic rings making their way into the ocean, harming the environment and sea life. That single move put Saltwater Brewery on the map; they blew the competition out of the water and built a global brand.

rt used to be in the news for all the wrong rea-
putation was of an unstoppable force destroying
ent retailers in small cities and towns while supporting sweat shops in faraway lands. In 2005 the CEO
and board of directors made a significant and conscious
shift to become an environmental leader and champion of
green supply chains. Walmart has regained significant social
license to operate as a result. Today the media rarely attacks
Walmart for its corporate practices. Rather, it reports on
the company's climate leadership.

A 2019 McKinsey study reported at least five proven
links to corporate performance and value creation from
ESG initiatives. The first is top-line growth. The study
revealed that "a strong ESG proposition helps companies tap new markets and expand into existing ones"[1] and
can substantially reduce costs, for example, energy and
water consumption costs. ESG can decrease regulatory and
legal interventions while increasing access to strategic and
friendly regulation and legislation. It can enhance employee
motivation, productivity, loyalty, and engagement. And
ESG attracts long-term investment and asset optimization.

The business case of ESG is undeniable.

Board members and c-suite executives are rapidly
becoming aware of ESG as an integrated way of looking
at corporate life. Yet many don't fully understand how it
affects their strategy and reporting at the board level or its
comprehensiveness and impacts.

What Is a Stakeholder?

Throughout this book, we will be referring to accountability towards stakeholders; therefore, we should be clear
on what is meant by a stakeholder. In a corporation, broadly
speaking, a *stakeholder* is a member of groups without whose
support the organization would cease to exist: its employees, customers, suppliers, creditors, and community. Your
stakeholders are at the heart of ESG.

Environment

We only have one earth. Individually and corporately, we are all stewards of the natural environment, but we have not protected, nurtured, or renewed it as well as we should have.

The good news is, while the pressure is on, it's not too late. Organizations can do both: be highly successful and save the planet at the same time!

Social

Social media has put immediate pressure on organizations to treat not only their employees but also their stakeholder groups with flawless integrity and justice. The ability for employees, consumers, clients, and others to report their experiences instantly and publicly with a particular business sets a high bar for organizations to live up to. The slightest slipup can do irreparable reputational damage.

There is good news here too! People are the soul of the organization—the spirit of the organization. When they are respected, valued, nurtured, and protected, both they and the organization are set up for success.

Governance

Many board members do not understand the complete governance system and their role within it. This lack of clarity leads to organizations that are not governed as well as they should be, thus weakening the organization and making it harder for it to compete.

Here is our third piece of good news. Well-governed companies outperform the competition.

In this book we

- explain what ESG is and why every board member and executive should care about it;

- cover how to measure ESG efforts and impacts;

- break E, S, and G down into easily understandable pieces of the larger ESG puzzle;

- give you an assessment tool to help you understand where you are on your own ESG journey; and

- demonstrate how ESG is your superpower for success in the boardroom!

Read on to learn how you can make more money, save the planet, empower people, gain social license, and outperform your competition as you set yourself up for long-term success.

CHAPTER 1

WHAT IS ESG AND WHY SHOULD I CARE?

What Is ESG?

Board members and c-suite executives are rapidly becoming aware of ESG as an integrated way of looking at corporate life rather than in separate streams. Many don't yet fully understand ESG, how it affects their strategy and reporting at the board level, or its comprehensiveness and impacts.

ESG refers to *environment, social,* and *governance* when measuring the sustainability and ethical impact of an investment in a business or company.

It is a generic term that is used primarily in capital markets where it originated. Investors commonly use ESG to evaluate the behavior of companies and determine an organization's future performance and thus their worth—their value. It covers the three main factors that socially responsible investors measure when deciding whether to invest in a company.

ESG makes sense because a responsible company that cares about its people, customers, and the environment is more likely to outperform its peers and be successful and resilient than one that does not. An ESG-based approach is more than just a way of attracting and retaining capital. It is much broader. At its core, embracing ESG is about doing the right thing.

ESG extends to organizations beyond those that are publicly traded. Any type of organization can benefit from an understanding and application of ESG. Donors, employees, and other stakeholders too consider ESG factors when deciding whether to donate, work for, or otherwise become engaged with an organization.

The E in ESG, or *environmental criteria*, includes the energy an organization takes in, the waste it discharges, the resources it needs, and the consequences for the planet and living beings as a result of an organization's activities. It encompasses issues such as carbon emissions and climate change. These are the best-known examples of the E of ESG. Every organization, from the sole proprietorship to the corporate giant, uses energy and resources. Every company affects, and is affected by, the environment. Consideration of ESG is not just for companies that are in oil and gas, energy, or extraction. We all have an environmental footprint, and there is something that all of us can do to improve our interactions with the environment.

The S in ESG, or *social criteria*, addresses the relationships an organization has and the reputation it fosters with people and institutions in the communities where it does business. *Social criteria* include elements like labor relations, diversity, equity, and inclusion. Every organization operates within a broader, diverse society. We call that *social license* or *social contract*. A social contract is a covenant. Without earning the social license to operate, a business will not reach its full potential. In a worst-case scenario, an organization will be prevented from moving forward if its leaders and employees abuse their relationship with a stakeholder.

The G in ESG, or *governance criteria*, is the system of direction and control of the organization. Governance criteria go further to include the operating system of practices, controls, policies, and procedures your company adopts to govern itself—to make effective decisions. It includes ethics, transparency, and going beyond complying with the letter of governing laws to fulfilling the spirit of them. Governance includes what is sometimes called *citizenship*: meeting the needs, expectations, and aspirations of external stakeholders and the public. Every organization requires governance, and the better an operation is governed, the more investment it will attract and the higher it will perform.

That is ESG 101!

Here's a real-world example to illustrate:

Let's talk about Tesla Inc. Many people, when they hear the word *Tesla*, think of electric cars. They think, "Good for the environment." They think, "Tesla must be a company that is an ESG company." They think, "Tesla must be a good company and therefore must be good to invest in." But is it? How does it stack up to ESG criteria?

MSCI is a company that assesses and provides ESG ratings for companies around the world so that investors can make informed investing choices. MSCI rated the electric vehicle producer, Tesla Inc., and this is what they found:

The company earns an overall grade of "A," putting it on the higher end of "average" among the 39 companies in the car industry rated by MSCI. Digging into its rating, Tesla excels in corporate governance and environmental risks, maintaining a relatively small carbon footprint and both utilizing and investing in green technologies. The company scores an average grade for product quality and safety, with the company making headlines in the past for exploding batteries, undesirable crash test ratings, and accidents involving the cars' self-driving "autopilot" feature—although CEO Elon Musk has publicly announced a commitment to improving both driver and bystander safety. What truly drags down Tesla's MSCI ESG rating is its below-average score for labor management practices. Tesla, for instance, has been found to be in violation of labor laws by blocking unionization, and it has violated the National Labor Relations Act multiple times. More recently, the company's leadership has come under fire for keeping plants open and unsafe during the COVID-19 pandemic, leading several of its workers to come down with the illness.[2]

So, according to this rating agency, Tesla rates well in the E and the G of ESG but loses important points in the S—the social criteria.

Sustainalytics, another influential rating organization, places Tesla in the high-risk category for investing in based on its ESG rating.

Compared to Fiat Chrysler, Honda, and Toyota, Tesla is a higher-risk investment based on its ESG ratings. In fact, Tesla ties with Ford as the riskiest ESG-based investments in the auto sector.

As we know, ESG has three streams; environment, social, and governance flow together when people decide whether to invest in a company or not. The view of several investor voices is that if a company fails the test on any of the three streams, it would not be considered an ESG investment. Therefore, some say[3] that Tesla is not an ESG investment because it does not pass on all three ESG streams.

One financial commentator echoes the thoughts of other internet bloggers that Tesla doesn't actually pass on the governance pillar either, based on independence—or lack thereof—of board members and on Elon Musk's compensation arrangements, which are not only significant but also not aligned with corporate results.

Companies cannot ignore the bloggers! Some rating organizations like Bloomberg and MSCI include metrics for social news sentiment scores. These organizations track news feeds daily for stories on companies' environmental and social behavior.

Tesla has skated along for some time on its reputation for putting the environment first, but its weak governance and what some call "horrid treatment of workers"[4] keeps it in the news for all the wrong reasons.

The point is this: when investors must make a choice between a leading, average, or lagging ESG-rated company, they will choose the leader every time.

Here's another illustration. When many people hear "BP Oil," they think of oil. They think, "Bad for the environment." They remember the Deepwater Horizon oil spill in the Gulf of Mexico, which began in April of 2010. They think, "BP Oil must be a company that is not an ESG company." They think, "BP Oil must be a bad company and therefore not good to invest in." But is it? How does BP Oil stack up to ESG criteria?

Turns out BP Oil is an ESG company. In fact, it rates strongly in all three categories: environment, social, and governance.

BP Oil's 2009 sustainability report was a typical communications piece. It is well-written. It positions the company as operating at the edge of the energy frontier and talks about how a revitalized BP is "driving innovative, efficient and responsible operations."[5] The report was barely posted on their website when the Deepwater Horizon disaster happened.

Fast forward to 2021. BP's 2021 sustainability report is night-and-day different from the 2009 report. The 2021 report is one hundred pages of full disclosure. It tells the reader not only what BP Oil wants people to know but also exactly how the company rates in multiple areas. The report is accompanied by a comprehensive datasheet of all their environmental metrics, and their website allows the public to drill into excel sheets to see what underlies the rolled-up information. Regardless of your thoughts on fossil fuels, there is no doubt that there has been a sea change at BP Oil, and it is serious about ESG.

The bottom line of these two stories is that Tesla is not considered an ESG company, but BP Oil is!

What Are the Drivers of ESG? Why Are We in the ESG Era?

Let's talk history. Over the last two decades, the following three streams have converged:

1. The first stream is the onset of environmentalism driven by both the science (for example, the impacts of climate change itself) and the voices of corporate and individual activists. Organizations (e.g., the United Nations and Greenpeace), political parties, individuals such as Al Gore, a plethora of celebrities, and of course the latest and perhaps loudest voice, Greta Thunberg, leading a force of student activities, have all worked to increase awareness of environmental issues. These examples barely scratch the surface of the voices calling out to protect our planet. Climate change protests have become a common occurrence and a driving force for action. The driver is of course the planet and human life itself. Collectively we only have one planet. Individually we only have one life. These facts are the true drivers of the environmentalist movement—the groans of

the planet and the realization of individuals that if we don't act, who will?

2. The second stream began with socially responsible investing (SRI) and was set off by a few niche players in the investment world, including union activists lobbying investors to do SRI. Faith-based organizations began calling for ethical and altruistic investment options. For example, SRI might mean not investing in companies that produce alcohol or tobacco or companies that produce morally questionable products. Or it could mean only investing in companies that have a proven track record of social responsibility and community investment.

Individual investors became increasingly frustrated at low returns on their retirement funds while a few individuals at the top were reaping exponentially large returns. At the same time, institutional investors were calling on corporations to consider the impacts on all corporate stakeholders rather than being solely focused on shareholder capitalism—on short-term financial returns. As a result, major institutional investors began taking a hard look at SRI.

SRI went from niche to mainstream quite quickly. The Occupy movement of 2011 expressed opposition to both social and economic inequality and sought to advance social justice. In less than a month, protestors rallied in over six hundred communities in the US alone and in almost a thousand cities across eighty-two countries.[6]

Additionally, two seminal documents were written that shook things up: one from the corporate community and the other from the investment community. In early 2012, Larry Fink, the CEO of

BlackRock, the world's largest asset management company, wrote an open letter to CEOs, an annual tradition that he has continued to this day. That first letter was a call to action, challenging corporations to adopt good governance and enhanced engagement with investors, with a focus on long-term performance.

Over the years, Fink's letters have built on his initial demands with an exhortation to meet stakeholder interests and resolve social and environmental issues. More recently his letters have included a challenge for corporations to prioritize climate change. In 2020 and 2021, he asked companies to disclose a plan for how their business model will be compatible with a net-zero economy and a method for how this plan will be incorporated into their long-term strategy and reviewed by their board of directors.

If one person can make a difference in the investment world, that one person is Larry Fink. As GlobeScan recently wrote, "BlackRock's annual CEO letters have become a rallying cry for responsible long-term business strategy."[7] What Larry Fink says, corporations do. His letters have directly resulted in corporate action in ESG. It is quite something!

Around the same time as Fink began writing his annual letters, Business Roundtable in the US published a paper about focusing less on short-term shareholder returns and more on sustainable returns, a similar but narrower theme than BlackRock's. The real driver here was that people were getting tired of what they saw as corporate greed and profit at the expense of the larger society and *the little guy*. Add to these streams the injustices brought to the fore by the #MeToo and Black Lives Matter movements, and we've got ourselves a real social and economic justice movement.

3. We can't forget the third stream, governance reform, which was set in motion by several large corporate failures in the early 1990s. This movement led to the question, "Where were the directors?" The case for governance reform came first from the Cadbury Report out of the UK, the King Report on Corporate Governance in South Africa, and the Dey Report in Canada. These were followed by the Sarbanes-Oxley Act in the US. Regulators and stock exchanges have since been setting new standards and rules for governance, reforming the way boards go about their work.

It is the confluence of these three streams which, like tributaries, flows into the raging river we call ESG: the planet screaming out to be saved and protected, *the little guy* screaming out for their savings and pensions to be saved and protected and not be eaten up by *the one percent*, and corporations themselves screaming out to be saved and protected.

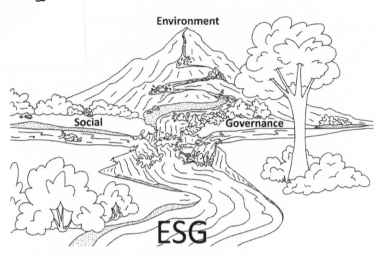

The corporation is a helpless child. It has a life in and of itself. It is begging to be protected, to be well-governed so that it can continue to live. The planet wants to live. People want to live. The corporation wants to live. These entities all want justice in their own way.

Enter the scene: ESG! It is a way of putting all the pieces together to save the planet, help people live healthy, productive, and resourced lives, and allow organizations to not just survive but thrive.

Perhaps as an organization twenty years ago, or maybe even as recently as ten, you could ignore any or all of these streams. The voices calling from the tributaries were distant. But those voices are now raging. Ignore them at your peril; you will be swept away by them.

How Is ESG Any Different Than CSR?

Some people think about ESG as simply an amped up corporate social responsibility (CSR) program, but by now you will have noticed that ESG is not the same as CSR. It is so much more. You can think of the distinction between CSR and ESG this way: *CSR* aims to make a business accountable; *ESG* criteria make the organization's efforts measurable. CSR is more about doing good in the community and reporting on what was done. ESG is CSR on steroids; it is applied and measured. It is broader and deeper, and its impacts are more visible and measurable.

In 1999 we (Debra and David) wrote a research paper published by The Conference Board of Canada called "When Leaders Serve: Engaging the Board in Corporate Social Responsibility."[8] At the time, many corporate executives thought of CSR as a fashionable trend that would help the corporation gain respect in the community—something to help them boost their brand and reputation. Corporations were finding that focusing strictly on profits was alienating their communities. They were starting to see how CSR might help them increase profits over the long term. Part of our research included surveying Canada's largest and leading corporations. Respondents told us the top five reasons they invested in CSR were that it

- creates a better workplace environment that attracts top talent;
- enhances productivity and thereby the bottom line;
- improves safety performance;
- raises corporate identity in the marketplace; and
- reflects the image of a well-run company.

While all good reasons to be good corporate citizens, these are all internally focused: we get good productive people to work for us, we do our best to keep them safe, we give to the community and people like us. The reasons focus on what's in it for the corporation. Traditional CSR falls short as it fails to realize that companies live on a two-way street. It is in the best interests of the corporation to look out for the interests of its stakeholders including the planet, the people, and the investors and owners. The relationship between corporation and stakeholder ought to be a win-win.

The rise of impact investing has led to the demand for ways to rank companies on their ESG performance, but at its heart, ESG is about creating a sustainable enterprise.

The concept of ESG is not just about altruism or the philanthropy of the CSR movement. ESG initiatives should provide material financial benefit to the organization. So, the question we ask about these programs is not just "How does ESG help our community or enhance our brand?" Beyond that, we seek to discern how we will create a sustainable organization—one that is sustainable for the planet, the people, and the companies (or profits), and one that has the resiliency to withstand the headwinds of economic turmoil and competition.

As Debra often says, "I am a *both/and* kind of girl!" ESG is not about *either/or*. It is about *both/and*. ESG programs and processes should benefit both society *and* your bottom line. They should have a positive impact on your corporate image *and* be designed for sustainability, including financial sustainability.

ESG is most effective when organizations look to their most material ESG-related risks and opportunities and effect change that will benefit both corporate reputation and financial returns. The work-from-home movement, for example, has brought positive measurable impacts to employee satisfaction and productivity while reducing negative impacts to the environment including greenhouse gas emissions.

What Are the Top Five Benefits of ESG for the Board?

Several important studies have found businesses that adopt ESG standards tend to be more conscientious, less risky, and consequently more likely to be successful over the long term. It is a myth to think that SRI comes at a cost—that you will make less money. In fact, the evidence tells us that the opposite is typically the case.

The first benefit people want to know about is the financial benefit. They ask, "How will this impact our bottom line?" The truth is investors look for companies with strong ESG. The number of investment funds that incorporate ESG factors into their investment decisions has been growing rapidly for some time now, and this trend is expected to continue.

The opposite is also true. If you have weak ESG, you will pay a premium to access capital. Strong ESG gives you better access to pools of capital, whether those are earmarked for ESG or they are mainstream investments. ESG investing is an increasing part of the capital market. The biggest investor in the world is BlackRock, and they are the single loudest investor voice supporting ESG initiatives and companies. Conversely, investors are less likely to support your company if you don't treat the environment and your people with the respect they deserve.

And the impact is felt not just on the investment side in terms of capital. ESG contributes directly to sales growth. Producing products that are sustainable attracts more customers and therefore increases sales. Customers are increasingly choosing sustainable products. If you are not keeping up with this trend, you will lose market share to your competitors who are. Your reputation will be negatively affected if you are perceived not to be *sustainable*, environmentally friendly, and socially responsible.

Another benefit for the bottom line lies in your processes. Expense reduction related to environmental efforts is measurable and meaningful (for example, reduced energy and water consumption and reduced waste generally). Packaging costs are driven down, as are waste disposal costs.

Higher-rated ESG companies have experienced increased productively. They are better able to attract, recruit, and retain highly-motivated talent due to alignment of social and environmental values. When there is a negative impression of your organization in the community, your talent pool diminishes. High-capacity people are less willing to work for a company that has little sense of purpose related to ESG issues.

The fifth key benefit ESG has on the bottom line is related to regulation. While regulation has been on the increase in environmental protections, many organizations have received significant subsidies and support from governments for introducing sustainable and pro-environmental initiatives. On the flip side, many others have experienced penalties and fines for not meeting stricter regulatory requirements, not to mention finding loss of favor with government and being subjected to more enforcement efforts enforcement efforts.

A good paradigm for thinking about how to report on your ESG initiatives is to use the balanced scorecard construct. There are likely many existing metrics in your balanced scorecard that you can use to begin to report on ESG if you are not already doing so. By using a framework you already have, you are not trying to reinvent the wheel. Most organizations already have some type of adapted balanced scorecard that provides a clear, easy lens that your stakeholders will be able to access and understand.

Balanced Scorecard Plus©	Benefits of High ESG	Negatives of Low ESG
1. FINANCIAL: Capital Investment	Investors look for companies with strong ESG. Companies have better access to pools of capital that are earmarked for ESG—this is an increasing part of the capital market. The biggest investor in the world is BlackRock, and they are the single biggest investor voice supporting ESG companies.	Investors are less likely to support your company.
2. CLIENT: Sales Growth	More sustainable products attract more customers, and therefore, sales increase.	Customers are attracted to and choose more sustainable products. Negative reputational perception exists.
3. PROCESS: Expense Reduction	Energy and water consumption decrease. Waste is reduced overall.	Packaging costs are higher. Waste disposal costs increase. Excessive waste is produced.
4. PEOPLE: Productivity	Companies attract, recruit, and retain highly motivated talent due to alignment of social and environmental values.	A negative impression in the community diminishes the talent pool. A weaker sense of purpose means the talent pool is less interested in working for the company.
5. ENVIRONMENT: Regulatory Benefits	Companies receive subsidies and support from governments for sustainable and pro-environmental efforts.	Companies incur penalties and fines for not meeting stricter regulatory requirements. Companies experience loss of favor with government and more enforcement.

Where Is ESG Going?

ESG is only going to gain more traction. It is not going away, and you ignore it at your peril.

In fact, there are some who are saying ESG is going to expand to ESGT, with the T meaning *technology*. This expansion would mean investors, customers, employees, and suppliers will be attracted to your company or repelled from it based on how you govern technology. For example, ESGT would include your approach to cybersecurity and data protection. What about data mining, the internet of things,[9] robotics and automated robotic processing, surveillance, and the handling of fake news? These are just some of the technological issues that people worry about, and they want the companies they buy from and work for to handle these issues responsibly.

It will not surprise us if a T gets added to ESG!

Environment	Social	Governance	Technology
Climate change	Human rights	Corporate governance	Cybersecurity
Sustainability	Labor rights	Leadership	AI geopolitics
Water	Child labor	Culture	Data mining
Air	Human trafficking	Business ethics	Internet of things
Earth	Human slavery	Geopolitics	Artificial intelligence
Carbon emissions	Health and safety	Corruption/bribery	Machine learning
Energy efficiency	Workplace conditions	Fraud	Deep learning
Natural resources	Workplace violence	Money laundering	Robotics
Hazardous waste	Product safety	Anti-competition/anti-trust	Automated robotic processing

Recycled material use	Fair trade	Regulatory compliance	Military robotics
Clean technology	Data privacy	Conflicts of interest	Surveillance
Green buildings	Discrimination	Compensation disclosure	Dark web
Biodiversity	Harassment		Fake news
Animal rights	Bullying		Deep fakes—visual
			Deep fakes—audio
Pandemics	Diversity and inclusion		Biometrics
			Wearables
			Nanotechnology
			Bioengineering
			Crispr

Source: World Economic Forum[10]

So What?

So, what does all of this this mean for you? What can you do?

First, here are a few a big-picture questions to ask around the boardroom table. These questions will keep you firmly focused on the governance roles of the board—direction and control.

Directional Question

- How confident are we that we have a fully integrated and financially material ESG program?

Control Questions

- How robust is our ESG reporting and disclosure? For example, does our organization produce a publicly available annual report detailing its ESG performance and results of ESG performance measures? If not, will we?

- How will we evaluate options for enhancing the materiality of our ESG program?

Some of you may have already asked and answered these questions in your management meetings or around your boardroom table. Some of you may not have. For many of you, reading this book may be the beginning of your ESG journey. Others may be well along the road and have a good grasp of these issues.

Regardless of where you are on your ESG journey, there will always be more you can do. We can have and support justice while profiting at the same time. ESG is a *both/ and* concept.

Second, you can assess your own ESG initiatives. At the end of this book, you will find the ESG Pulse Check Assessment for Boards (Appendix 1), which we created to help you do this self-assessment. The results of such an assessment will show you where you are doing well and where you will want to focus your efforts.

Together we can quiet the screams of our planet, people, and organizations and traverse the raging river of ESG. As our world emerges from the COVID-19 crisis, the environment and social justice movements will only add more and more water to the tributaries feeding the river. We are convinced that our corporate lives and social covenant will be changed forever in a post-COVID world. That change will be for the good in terms of our care for stakeholders, long-term sustainability, and desire to become and remain responsible corporate citizens.

CHAPTER 2
HOW THE E OF ESG HELPS BOARDS SAVE THE PLANET

The natural environment must be protected,
nurtured, and renewed.

—Dr. Debra L. Brown

Let's start by pointing out the obvious. We only have one earth. Just one. That beautiful blue planet that hangs in space. It is ours to live on, benefit from, and care for. Collectively and individually, we are stewards of this incredible natural environment. The problem is, we have not protected, nurtured, and renewed it as well as we could or should have.

Why is that?

Here are our top six reasons:

1. **Short-termism:** We think the world has endless resources and the ability to renew itself. We are more concerned about what we can get now versus the impacts our consumption will have on the next generation.

2. **Irresponsibility:** Many have not taken up the responsibility of being stewards of the natural environment, and in fact we do worse; we cause harm to our planet. Caring for the earth is no longer a recommendation but an urgent requirement.

3. **Greed and Selfishness:** We focus on either saving money or making financial gain at the expense of the environment. For example, many are not willing to pay a bit extra for an electric or fuel-efficient car even when it is within their ability to do so.

4. **Apathy:** Apathy means having a lack of concern. Many people just don't care about the earth. They don't see how big-picture environmental issues impact their day-to-day life and are therefore apathetic toward caring for it.

5. **A preference for ease:** Human beings prefer ease. For example, it is easier to dump our trash in the ocean—out of sight, out of mind—than it is to purchase property and manage waste responsibly.

6. **Values:** The value placed on the natural environment and on human life differs from person to person, community to community, and nation to nation. We would also posit that it is linked to how we value ourselves. When we understand that each of us matters, that each of us adds value to the world, then

we realize that one person and one person's actions matter. Your actions matter. Your big actions and your small ones can all make a difference, whether that is mowing your lawn with a gas mower or a push mower! Together, the little steps we take as individuals add up to big results.

Hopefully, the world is waking up to what is happening all around us. We can no longer pretend that certain situations don't exist or have nothing to do with our lives. What happens in the east affects the west and vice versa.

The truth is, organizations can do both; they can be highly successful and save the planet at the same time!

Here's the good news. Corporations of all types are combating

1. **short-termism** with longer-term views of their outputs and the impacts of those outputs. For example, consider the efforts of Larry Fink of BlackRock. He focused the minds and actions of corporations on adding long-term value over short-term profits.

2. **irresponsibility** by being accountable for their environmental choices and the subsequent impacts. They are putting programs together and going public with their efforts.

3. **greed and selfishness** by finding ways to save the environment and have positive impacts on it while at the same time growing their businesses and reinvesting in people and planet. They are recognizing that reinvestment creates profit.

4. **apathy** by increasing their awareness of the negative impacts they have had. Organizations are waking up and listening to the watchdogs, their employees,

customers, and communities. Empathy for people and planet is replacing apathy. When we are encouraged in our workplaces to have empathy for people and planet, we carry those values home into our private lives.

5. **preference for ease** and replacing it with investments of time, money, and energy. People are doing the hard work of environmental stewardship. Many organizations are no longer taking the easy path.

6. **values** that do not support a healthy environment. Global organizations and governments are pressuring business and nations to step up and place the value on the environment that it deserves. Internally people are becoming aware of their impact on the environment, and the added external pressure is causing organizations to up their game.

Our first point in this chapter is that the environment matters. We only have one earth. It needs to be protected, nurtured, and renewed. It has suffered extreme harm from business, industry, and consumers for far too long, and we can no longer ignore its groanings. We cannot ignore environmental laws. Change is in the wind.

How Can and Should Businesses Be Stewards of the Natural Environment?

This aspect of ESG concentrates on environmental criteria which examines how a business performs as a steward of our natural environment. The primary focus is on

- waste and pollution;
- resource depletion;

- greenhouse gas emission;
- deforestation; and
- climate change.

In the last chapter, we mentioned an ESG Pulse Check Assessment for Boards at the end of this book. This assessment asks you ten questions related to the environment. These are the top ten areas that boards are thinking about:

1. Does your board receive metrics on the organization's contribution to climate change?

2. Does your organization have a proactive antipollution and waste management policy?

3. Does your organization use and invest in green technology in meaningful ways?

4. Does your organization replenish energy at a rate that is equal to or faster than the rate at which it is consumed?

5. Is your organization housed in green buildings and facilities?

6. Does your organization have a target to have a carbon neutral footprint that it is actively pursuing?

7. Does your organization handle hazardous waste in a way that it is collected, stored, transported, treated, recovered, and disposed of to reduce adverse effects to human health and the environment?

8. Does your organization have a policy for its water use with an aim toward conservation?

9. Does your organization do everything it can to avoid resource depletion?

10. Does your organization have a policy to use recycled or reused materials as a first and best choice option?

We have a saying in governance: you don't just get what you plan; you get what you plan, recourse, measure, and reward. This ten-point checklist is an intentional way of getting to the key elements of an environmental sustainability strategy and therefore measures how we might monitor and evaluate that strategy.

Case Study: The World Economic Forum

The World Economic Forum's mission statement outlines that the Forum "engages the foremost political, business, cultural and other leaders of society to shape global, regional and industry agendas."[11] So, what does the Forum do? It does research and brings people together to talk about issues. It holds a lot of meetings. The Forum's website states that "while aiming to make its summits more sustainable, the Forum is also working to improve the sustainability of its offices, global operations and business processes."[12]

Here are ten steps the Forum takes to be more sustainable. These are steps that most organizations could easily take as well:

1. **They have Leadership in Energy and Environmental Design (LEED)-certified offices:** The Forum's 2021 sustainability strategy requires that the design and build of new Forum offices be LEED-certified and integrate the most stringent sustainability standards. For example, the Forum's New York, Beijing, and San Francisco offices are rated platinum or gold LEED-certified.

2. **They actively promote sustainable green spaces:** The Forum has ceased the use of chemicals, thereby

optimizing the water resources needed to maintain green spaces. They have recently introduced more green spaces, including diverse flowering lawns and larger indigenous hedges, at their headquarters. They have also installed wildlife shelters such as houses for birds and insects.

3. **They ensure sustainable catering:** In Geneva, the Forum provides food and drink daily to its employees, visitors, and meeting participants. They have developed institutional catering guidelines in order to ensure that their commitment to sustainability is front and center. Their goal is to curb loss and waste as much as possible while producing adequate quantities of food. They also aim to create value for local communities through engagement with producers or local suppliers and by supporting fair working conditions and employee well-being along the value chain. They place a strong emphasis on sourcing fresh, local, and organic produce.

4. **They implement a paper-reduction plan:** One of the Forum's main goals is to limit their use of paper. For special occasions, the Forum produces publications, which are cradle-to-cradle certified. This certification guarantees that all raw products used in the production of their publications can be returned to the biological cycle without causing any harm to the natural environment.

5. **They are moving away from single-use plastic:** Single-use plastic containers are no longer used for serving beverages at their Geneva offices. In conjunction with their events production company, the Forum also works to replace single-use plastic wrapping with greener alternatives.

6. **They are committed to energy leadership:** The Forum has set goals to reduce their energy consumption. For example, in spite of an increased number of employees, the Geneva offices reduced their consumption by 23 percent from 2015 to 2018 by carefully monitoring and investing in energy-efficient equipment.

7. **They encourage sustainable commuting:** The Forum's sustainability strategy includes an emphasis on using sustainable transport, such as walking and biking, for commuting. They have provided electric bicycles for employee use, installed additional bicycle parking spaces at the Geneva headquarters, and offered subsidies to employees who use public transportation. As one example of the results of their efforts, employees saved 1.8 tons of carbon dioxide (CO_2) in one month by participating in the Swiss Bike to Work challenge.

8. **They use renewable energy:** The Forum uses only 100 percent renewable energy for the electricity in the building. Geothermal energy and heat pumps provide 100 percent of the energy for air heating and cooling of the main building, and heat recovery from kitchen equipment heats the water used throughout the building.

9. **They adopted responsible sourcing:** The Forum's Sustainable Procurement Policy was adopted in 2017. The driving force behind the policy is to place emphasis on conducting business with conscientious suppliers—those who demonstrate recognition of their environmental responsibilities by respecting the rule of law and human rights and making conscious choices about the products and materials they supply.

10. **They foster recycling:** Forum offices in Geneva, New York, and San Francisco no longer use individual desk bins. Instead, shared waste-sorting stations are stationed throughout workspaces with the aim of heightening employee awareness on waste and improving the quality of the waste sorting, thereby increasing recycling rates.[13]

Some business leaders see themselves as a small fish in a big ocean and therefore believe their environmental efforts will not make a difference on a global scale. But this events-based think tank, The World Economic Forum, does what it can within its sphere of control and influence to protect the natural environment, and in the process, it saves money.

Caring for the environment is a fast-growing area of concern for boards. They want to know what the organization is doing to help reduce their carbon footprint. Boards want to understand what the organization's waste levels are and therefore determine where the organization's impact on the planet can be lessened, or at the very least, made neutral over time and, at the very best, improved. The ultimate goal is to better the natural environment over time.

Different Types of Businesses Will Have a Different Materiality Threshold

Depending on the type of organization you are in, your materiality threshold will differ.

For instance, environmental impacts are far more material to heavy industry or delivery services than they are to a financial services company or a local charitable organization. That doesn't mean that all types of organization can't find ways to reduce their impact on the environment; it just means that the materiality of their efforts, both to internal efficiencies and external impacts, are relative. A delivery service that optimizes routes or invests in electric vehicles will see far higher returns, but the local service club that installs LED lighting will also benefit.

Case Study: Amazon

Front and center on Amazon's website is its public statement related to the planet: "We are committed to and invested in sustainability because it's a win all around—it's good for the planet, for business, for our customers, and for our communities."[14]

They go on to make four statements:

1. The first is Amazon's climate pledge—its commitment to be net-zero carbon by 2040. It is on pace to be using, by 2025, 100 percent renewable energy to power its operations.

2. Its second statement, pertaining to sustainable operations, outlines the commitments Amazon has made to building a sustainable business for its customers, communities, and the world by such actions as reducing water usage in data centers and using sustainable aviation fuel.

3. Third is its statement related to its supply chain. Amazon has committed to working closely with its suppliers to communicate environmental standards and help suppliers build their capacity to provide working environments that are safe and respectful of human rights.

4. Fourth, Amazon is committed to improved packaging. It is working to invent packaging that will eliminate waste while ensuring products arrive intact and undamaged.[15]

Some people love to hate Amazon and even its founder, but the truth is, leaders at Amazon are working hard to reduce their environmental impacts, and they have important targets and metrics that they are resourcing, measuring, and reporting on both to the board and publicly. The four points above are just a fraction of the efforts Amazon is making as it implements its environmental agenda.

Not All News Is Good News

The news stories we hear about the environment are not always positive. Where we live in Toronto, Canada, recently there have been news reports on our national television networks related to toxic chemicals in products at some of our favorite places to eat and shop.

Here is one example from CTV News: 'Tim Hortons, Metro among retailers in new report's toxic chemicals 'hall of shame.'"[16]

An organization out of the US called *Safer Chemicals Healthy Families* was founded in 2009 by Andy Igrejas to create a coalition of hundreds of organizations and businesses.[17] The goal of the coalition is to tackle the problem of unsafe chemicals leaching into the environment and therefore into our bodies. That organization has created a program called *Mind the Store*.[18] The program provides a report card on retailers in the US and Canada, evaluating their use of toxic chemicals in their products and packaging.

This year, their fifth year of producing the report card, Mind the Store rated over two hundred thousand stores across hundreds of major brands. Fifteen brands received a grade of F. Three major Canadian brands—Metro, Sobeys, and Tim Hortons—were in that group of fifteen. In comparison, Apple and Target scored A+, each of them earning more than one hundred points. Metro, on the other hand, did not even get one point!

The report revealed that "there is no indication that Metro has made any significant public-facing commitments to address the safety of chemicals used in the products it sells, including any indirect food additives that may be in food contact materials."[19]

Of Sobeys, it said there was no indication that it is taking action to address the issue of toxic indirect food additives, chemicals, and certain plastics.[20]

And of Restaurant Brands International, the parent company of Canada's beloved Tim Hortons, the report card states it "has no significant public-facing commitments to address the safety of indirect food additives that may be in food contact materials."[21] It also said, however, "the company does receive credit for restricting various chemicals of high concern in promotional toys, for restricting bisphenol A (BPA) in food-contact materials, and for setting a goal to eliminate expanded polystyrene foam in all food packaging globally by 2021."[22]

Tim Hortons tried to defend its reputation to the media, but the damage of the headline was done. The phrases *Tim Hortons* and *toxic chemicals* are now linked in the minds of consumers. Within three weeks of the release of the scathing news article, Tim Hortons launched a major national ad campaign in an attempt to redeem its reputation as it related to the environment.

Subway, Starbucks, Burger King, and Popeyes also rated F, as did Nordstrom and 7-11.

So what's my point? You can't just get by on good coffee! You need to be a responsible corporate citizen. People are watching. The people who work for you are watching, as are those who buy your products and the communities in which you operate. And there are watchdogs out there. Organizations are watching what you do, and they will report on your actions or your inaction. You could be the next Tim Hortons! Organizations simply must be accountable to the natural environment and the people who live in it.

What Are the Legal and Financial Implications for Directors When it Comes to Environmental Issues?

Firstly, let's talk about the personal liability an individual board member may have because of environmental impact. There are two different ways that you can be personally liable as a board member. One is if you breach your statutory duties of loyalty or care, the most common example of which is an undisclosed conflict of interest or a breach of confidentiality. The other is if a particular statute or act of a jurisdiction states that a director may be held personally liable in certain instances. Environmental protection legislation is one of those statutes where there is a direct exception. Even if you don't breach your duties of loyalty and care, you can still be held liable. Therefore, there are legal and financial implications for directors when it comes to environmental issues. For example, in North America, directors have been held liable for environmental issues related to the actions of their corporations.

Beyond that, investors are increasingly looking for enhanced environmental reporting from issuers. They can and have punished the stock prices of corporations that have poor performance on environmental issues. Donors reduce or cease giving to not-for-profits and charities that ignore environmental issues. And employees prefer to work for organizations that show themselves to be environmentally conscientious. The question at hand is not just about climate change; environmental programs go well beyond carbon footprints. Well-conceived programs will protect long-term assets, stakeholder relationships, employee recruitment and retention, and corporate reputation.

Environmental sustainability and impact get the attention of courts, creating litigation and liability, and therefore have a great deal of associated risk. It's not surprising then that of all the layers of CSR, sustainability is usually the one that comes to the board's attention first and holds the board's attention longest because of the risk and potential liability to the organization and the individual directors.

What Role Can and Should the Board Play?

Any board should review its strategic plan to ensure some level of environmental program relative to its industry and environmental impacts. If environmental impact doesn't get raised to the level of strategy, it is almost impossible for a board to have line of sight to that impact. If you are concerned that environmental sustainability is not a strategic consideration in your organization, here are a couple of basic questions you can ask management to get the conversation started:

1. How confident are we that we have implemented environmentally friendly programs?

2. Are we compliant with all environmental regulations?

3. Have we set targets related to our environmental programs, and are we reviewing results against these at the board level?

Depending on how those questions are answered, you may either be satisfied the organization is on track, or you may find out there is some work to be done!

If you are farther down the road, go deeper and take the ESG Pulse Check Assessment at the end of this book (Appendix 1).

What Generally Accepted Protocols and Guidelines for Environmental Reporting and Disclosure Should Boards Be Aware Of?

There are generally accepted protocols and guidelines for environmental reporting and disclosure. The Carbon Disclosure Project (CDP) is an important example. CDP is an international not-for-profit that runs the global disclosure system for investors, companies, cities, states, and regions to manage their environmental impacts. Each year, CDP takes the information supplied in its annual reporting process and scores companies and cities based on their disclosures in environmental leadership. They measure corporate and city progress on climate change, forests, and water security.[23] Across the board in ESG reporting, you don't need to reinvent the wheel; you can adopt and implement global codes sized to your needs and aspirations.

Global Reporting Initiative (GRI)

GRI is an independent international organization which helps businesses understand and communicate their impact on critical sustainability issues such as climate change, human rights, governance, and social well-being. Their mission is to "enable organizations to be transparent and take responsibility for their impacts, enabled through the world's most widely used standards for sustainability reporting."[24]

GRI's core product is "The GRI Standards: The Global Standards for Sustainability Reporting,"[25] which is made available as a free public good. These standards cover topics ranging from "anticorruption to water, biodiversity to occupational health and safety, tax to emissions"[26] and have been continuously developed over twenty years.

The GRI Standards are the first global standards for sustainability reporting. They represent global best practices for reporting on a range of economic, environmental, and social impacts. The GRI Standards are also the most widely adopted global standards for sustainability reporting (93 percent of the world's largest 250 corporations report on their sustainability performance).[27]

You can access the GRI Standards here: globalreporting. org/standards/download-the-standards.

GRI is designed for larger companies. If you are a small company, you may benefit from a slice of these standards, but some of the other standards we mention below would be a better fit for you.

AccountAbility

AccountAbility is another standard-setting organization. It is one of the oldest of the external protocols for environmental stewardship. AccountAbility's AA1000 Series of Standards are principles-based frameworks used by global businesses, private enterprises, governments, and other public and private organizations to demonstrate leadership and performance in accountability, responsibility, and sustainability. AccountAbility is also recognized as the framework developer for the World Economic Forum's ESG Ecosystem Map,[28] which acknowledges the impact of the AA1000 Series of Standards in advancing large-scale, integrated, and focused ESG change.

The AA1000 Series of Standards include simple, practical, and easy-to-use frameworks for

1. developing, analyzing, and implementing sustainability initiatives (AA1000AP, 2018);

2. creating and conducting inclusive sustainability-related stakeholder engagement practices (AA1000SES, 2015); and

3. assuring credibility in reporting on progress toward sustainability goals (AA1000AS v3).

All three AccountAbility AA1000 Standards are available for free download at accountability.org/standards.

Greenhouse Gas (GHG) Protocol

GHG Protocol establishes comprehensive global standardized frameworks to measure and manage greenhouse gas emissions from private and public sector operations, value chains, and mitigation actions.

The Greenhouse Gas Protocol: A Corporate Accounting and Reporting Standard provides requirements and guidance for companies and other organizations preparing a corporate-level GHG emissions inventory. The Standard covers the accounting and reporting of seven greenhouse gases covered by the Kyoto Protocol: carbon dioxide (CO_2), methane (CH_4), nitrous oxide (N_2O), hydrofluorocarbons (HFCs), perfluorocarbons (PFCs), sulfur hexafluoride (SF_6), and nitrogen trifluoride (NF_3). It was updated in 2015 with the Scope 2 Guidance, which allows companies to credibly measure and report emissions from purchased or acquired electricity, steam, heat, and cooling.[29]

The first edition of the Standard, published in 2001, has been updated with additional guidance that clarifies how companies can measure emissions from electricity and other energy purchases and account for emissions from throughout their value chains. GHG Protocol also developed a suite of calculation tools to assist companies in calculating their greenhouse gas emissions and measure the benefits of climate change mitigation projects.

"In 2016, 92% of Fortune 500 companies responding to the CDP used GHG Protocol directly or indirectly through a program based on GHG Protocol."[30]

United Nations (UN) Sustainability Goals

The UN Sustainability Goals are the simplest and the most intuitive of the protocols and guidelines we have mentioned this far. They cover all of ESG, not just E (environment). There are seventeen goals in total, all of which have been adopted by the UN.[31]

One country that has fully adopted these goals is Canada. You can learn about Canada's action on these goals on the Government of Canada website.[32] You will see that Canada's sustainability goals exactly mirror those of the UN.

These seventeen goals are much more macro in nature than those of the GRI, AccountAbility, and the GHG, which are quite micro in nature when it comes to corporate application. The UN Sustainability Goals serve as a helpful checklist for organizations that want to make a difference in ESG.

Here are the seventeen UN Sustainability Goals:

1. **No Poverty:** End poverty in all of its forms everywhere.

2. **Zero Hunger:** End hunger, achieve food security and improved nutrition, and promote sustainable agriculture.

3. **Good Health and Well-being:** Ensure healthy lives and promote well-being for all at all ages.

4. **Quality Education:** Ensure inclusive and equitable quality education and promote lifelong learning opportunities for all.

5. **Gender Equality:** Achieve gender equality and empower all women and girls.

6. **Clean Water and Sanitation:** Ensure availability and sustainable management of water and sanitation for all.

7. **Affordable and Clean Energy:** Ensure access to affordable, reliable, sustainable, and modern energy for all.

8. **Decent Work and Economic Growth:** Promote sustained, inclusive, and sustainable economic growth, full and productive employment, and decent work for all.

9. **Industry, Innovation and Infrastructure:** Build resilient infrastructure, promote inclusive and sustainable industrialization, and foster innovation.

10. **Reduced Inequalities:** Reduce inequality within and among countries.

11. **Sustainable Cities and Communities:** Make cities and human settlements inclusive, safe, resilient, and sustainable.

12. **Responsible Consumption and Production:** Ensure sustainable consumption and production patterns.

13. **Climate Action:** Take urgent action to combat climate change and its impacts.

14. **Life Below Water:** Conserve and sustainably use the oceans, seas, and marine resources for sustainable development.

15. **Life on Land:** Protect, restore, and promote sustainable use of terrestrial ecosystems, sustainably manage forests, combat desertification, halt and reverse land degradation, and halt biodiversity loss.

16. **Peace, Justice and Strong Institutions:** Promote peaceful and inclusive societies for sustainable development, provide access to justice for all, and build effective, accountable, and inclusive institutions at all levels.

17. **Partnerships for the Goals:** Strengthen the means of implementation and revitalize the global partnership for sustainable development.[33]

The Global Carbon Project (GCP)

"The GCP integrates knowledge of greenhouse gases for human activities and the Earth system. [Their] projects include global budgets for three dominant greenhouse gases—carbon dioxide, methane, and nitrous oxide—and complementary efforts in urban, regional, cumulative, and negative emissions."[34]

The scientific goal of the GCP is to develop a complete picture of the global carbon cycle, including both its biophysical and human dimensions together with the interactions and feedbacks between them. The complete picture includes the following pieces:

- **Patterns and Variability:** What are the current geographical and temporal distributions of the major pools and fluxes in the global carbon cycle?

- **Processes and Interactions:** What are the control and feedback mechanisms—both anthropogenic and nonanthropogenic—that determine the dynamics of the carbon cycle?

- **Carbon Management:** What are the dynamics of the carbon-climate-human system moving into the future, and what points of intervention and windows of opportunity exist for human societies to manage this system?

The protocols outlined above (those provided by GRI, AccountAbility, GHG, the UN, and GCP) are some of the best known international protocols that you can apply to help inform how you might measure, monitor, and evaluate your corporate environmental footprint. Don't try to adopt them all! Don't even try to adopt even one of them fully right away! Implementing such protocols and meeting the targets you set for your organization will be a journey. If you haven't already, have your management team pick the one guideline that works the best for you, and get started on the journey.

Those Who Rate/Assess You!

What about those who assess you? The watchdogs! As we discussed in the last chapter, there are organizations that review and assess the environmental impacts of corporations. The CDP is one such organization.

CDP

CDP is a not-for-profit charity that runs the global disclosure system for investors, companies, cities, states, and regions in order to manage their environmental impacts. "The world's economy looks to CDP as the gold standard of environmental reporting with the richest and most comprehensive dataset on corporate and city action."[35] For twenty years, CDP has been scoring companies and countries on their environmental impact. For example, they give Amazon an F despite the efforts we have already highlighted. And Starbucks gets a D while Walmart earns an A, which makes one wonder, why is that? What is it that Walmart does that these others don't in terms of their carbon emissions?

MSCI

MSCI has been providing decision support tools and services for the global investment community for over fifty years. Their expertise is in research, data, and technology. According to their website, they

> power better investment decisions by enabling clients to understand and analyze key drivers of risk and return and confidently build more effective portfolios and create industry-leading, research enhanced solutions that clients use to gain insight into and improve transparency across the investment process.[36]

They now track a company's ESG efforts using an ESG framework. Those looking to invest in your company will check your MSCI rating before making their decision.

Sustainalytics

Sustainalytics' ESG Risk Ratings "offer clear insights into the ESG risks of companies."[37] They support hundreds of the world's foremost investors who incorporate ESG and corporate governance insights into their investment processes.

BlackRock is an example of a corporation that uses both Sustainalytics and MSCI.

Other proxy advisors use their own evaluation grids and metrics in addition to relying on MSCI and Sustainalytics.

What Is The Long and Short of the E of ESG?

The various protocols and rating agencies that we have highlighted in this chapter do not present an exhaustive list. For example, we don't want to forget the retailer report card that called out Tim Hortons! They are getting a big following these days. What we have presented are the most well-known and the best examples to illustrate the depth and breadth of the various protocols in play.

We cannot forget, too, that the media, consumer groups, or individual social media posts as self-appointed experts can come out of the blue and rate you on any aspect of your ESG! To the extent you can be proactive and tell your story, you should do so. It may not be enough to blunt the impacts of these sorts of assessments, but at least you have your message ready so that you can be proactive.

Here is the long and short of the E of ESG:

1. The environment matters; it must be protected, nurtured, and renewed.

2. Any business of any size or type can be and is a steward of the natural environment; everyone can do something.

3. Different types of businesses will have different materiality thresholds and issues related specifically to their operations.

4. There are legal and financial implications for directors when it comes to environmental issues, and these are only going to continue to increase.

5. The board can and should play a role in overseeing an organization's environmental stewardship and impact.

6. There are generally accepted protocols and guidelines for environmental reporting and disclosure the board should be aware of.

We end this chapter with a story about a small local curling club. This small-town club had an ice plant that was working just fine, but it leaked chlorofluorocarbons (CFCs). As one member of the club said, "We had our own hole in the ozone that we were creating right over the curling club." The board of the club decided that this problem was not something they could live with. They initiated a fundraiser and raised enough money to replace the ice plant. A couple of years later, they replaced all the lighting with LED lighting. While LED lighting has a payback, it is a lengthy one. Changing over to LED didn't make business sense. However, the club did so to be a good corporate citizen in their community.

This is just one example of small efforts from a small organization that made the biggest impact they could within their own sphere of control and influence.

No one large corporation doing everything they need to do will be able to change the trajectory of damage that humanity has inflicted on our natural environment. But together, all of us can.

CHAPTER 3

HOW THE S OF ESG GIVES YOUR ORGANIZATION ITS SOCIAL LICENSE

If environment is about recognizing that the environment matters, then social, the S of ESG, is about recognizing that people matter! People are the soul of the organization—the spirit of the organization, which must be nurtured, protected, and renewed for it to succeed.

Every organization is a person under the law—a corporate body. The board is the directing mind of that body, and the people who work for the organization are its soul. We would go so far as to say an organization's customers, suppliers, and communities too—any person that the corporation impacts in some social way—are part of the corporate soul. They all should matter to the organization.

What Is a Social License and How Do We Get One?

Social license consists of the extent and reach of an organization's contribution to society—the society that gives it permission to operate from the perspective of the communities it touches. Social license is the unwritten covenant we have with all our stakeholders to operate. It is an umbrella concept.

Some writers on the subject describe social license as being intangible and unwritten.[38] Others say that it is "difficult if not impossible to measure."[39] As time has gone on, however, organizations are getting better at understanding what social license is and how to measure it.

Over time, the subjects included in what is meant by social license have expanded. In general, there are three streams or overarching issues that feed into social license:

1. social responsibility;

2. social rights; and

3. social justice.

The roots of social license as a term or concept can be found in the mining sector. It appeared in the mid-1990s from within the industry as mining companies began to respond to social risk. The focus of their efforts to build social license in the communities they operated in was centered on three themes: legitimacy, credibility, and trust. Their logic was that "as a mining operation develops legitimacy and then credibility with its local stakeholders, acceptance and then approval of the operation will follow."[40]

In other words, if we operate in a community, we are part of that community. We will listen to the community, care for, protect, and invest in it. We will clean up after ourselves while we are there, and if we leave, we redevelop and/or restore before we go. We will be a trustworthy member of that community. Like a contract, social license is always two-sided. There is a give and get—a reciprocity that takes place. It is a value exchange between the company and the community. Social license is rarely written as a legal agreement. It is more of an understanding—a social contract that is expected or a covenant.

Let's look at the three parts of the social license: social responsibility, rights, and justice.

Social Responsibility

In early December 1984, there was a disastrous explosion in Bhopal, Madhya Pradesh, India at a pesticide plant operated by Union Carbide, a large private sector company.

The signs of trouble were evident long before the disaster happened. Lots of signs.

Eight years earlier, in 1976, there had been complaints about pollution. In 1981 there was a death of an employee from a pesticide leak. Investigators warned that the community was living on the edge of a volcano. From 1982 through 1984, there were several more serious incidents that caused deaths and poisonings, and in one case, an employee received burns over 30 percent of his body.

The explosion on the night of December 2, 1984, caused a highly toxic gas to be released, which spread across a densely populated area. Over 2,200 people died immediately. The final death toll was just under 3,800. However, over half a million people were injured, with 4,000 of those permanently so. Those are the official numbers. Some estimate numbers were even higher than this.

Union Carbide claimed the explosion was an act of sabotage. The Indian government and others in the community claimed the cause was lax management and poor pipe maintenance. Based on the company's history and subsequent investigations, it was clearly the latter.

It took years to unravel and clean up the aftermath. By June of 2010, seven Indian nationals, including the chair of Union Carbide India, were convicted of causing death by negligence.[41] They paid a $2,000 fine and were sentenced to two years in prison. They were all released immediately after being sentenced.

Regardless of the cause, Union Carbide had written legal agreements—formal covenants—with its shareholders, creditors, lenders, and employees. But what about the community in which it operated? What about the covenant it had with the community?

There was no written agreement, no formal covenant to look back to with respect to holding the company accountable. Their unwritten covenant with the community asserted that if there was a leak, a siren would sound in the community and residents would know to leave the area.

The night of the disaster, employees made several poor judgments, one of which was to wait and have teatime before checking into a warning that pressure was building in the tanks. They came back from tea to discover the pressure had gone past the point of no return. They decided that they did not want to wake and alarm area residents, so they purposefully turned off the siren as soon as it started to sound. The cost of that decision to the community is almost unspeakable. But the worst of their actions was to break that unwritten social covenant; they broke their covenant with the community.

The Bhopal disaster led to worldwide soul-searching in terms of social license. It forced companies to consider what the contract between a company and the community in which it operates should be.

The Bhopal disaster is seen as a watershed moment in social license. This horrible incident led to the mining sector coining the phrase *social license* and to the broader understanding of it that we have today.

Social Rights

When it comes to human rights, there was a watershed moment in Canada on June 26, 2014.

The Supreme Court of Canada made a landmark decision on a case about Indigenous rights involving the Tsilqhot'in Nation (pronounced Sil-KO-tin) in British Columbia. That case ruled that Indigenous people have a natural title to land even if they don't have a written treaty signed by the Crown.

The Court held that Aboriginal title constitutes a beneficial interest in the land, the underlying control of which is retained by the Crown. Natural rights conferred by Aboriginal title include the right to decide how the land will be used; to enjoy, occupy, and possess the land; and to proactively use and manage the land, including its natural resources. However, the Court set out a mechanism by which the Crown can override Aboriginal title if it deems it to be in the public interest, but the Crown can't unilaterally do that. It must have carried out consultation and accommodation. Its actions must have been supported by a compelling and substantial objective, and its actions must be consistent with its fiduciary obligation to the Indigenous people in question.[42]

That watershed ruling confirms what social license means today as it relates to social rights. If you want to operate on Indigenous land, whether to build a mine or install a hydro line, you must engage in meaningful consultation with the people who have natural title to the land. The title holders do not need to consent to the plans of the company, but meaningful consultation must take place. To this they have a right.

In Canada, Indigenous rights are a significant consideration companies must make. This is not an option; you must engage in these consultations. All of us that are part of companies that operate on lands where Indigenous people have natural title are navigating what it means to actively and meaningfully consult and accommodate to extend our social license. This is probably our clearest example of human rights and social rights as they relate to social license.

Social Justice

The third aspect of social license is *social justice*.

There is a tremendous call for all of us, individually and corporately, to take a more proactive approach to social justice.

It used to be that if you owned a company that operated globally, if you followed the higher of either your own country's standards or those of the country you were operating in, even if you didn't have to, you were a good corporate citizen acting in a socially just manner.

From our own experience, many years ago we led meetings about CSR for The Conference Board of Canada. In those days, the mid-1990s, Canadian companies that followed Canadian employee health and safety laws wherever they were in the world were the exception and seen as best in class.

Social justice is so much more proactive than that today.

Social justice is about actively protecting and championing the human rights of your employees and other stakeholders. It begins with issues such as sexual abuse and harassment in the workplace but quickly broadens out to encompass equity, diversity, and inclusion (EDI).

The social justice movement has expanded to the point that organizations are hiring c-suite EDI leads and considering EDI board committees; EDI has spawned its own industry. There are EDI professors and university courses, consultants, and master trainers, among others. We (David and Debra) are reminded of when we first became governance consultants. At the time, thirty years ago, there were three of us in Canada doing governance: Patrick O'Callaghan and the two of us. Governance is now a full-fledged global industry. The governance industry was spawned by governance failures and the realization that boards of directors were asleep at the switch. In the same way, the EDI industry has been spawned by new and heightened realizations of the injustices that are taking place all around us.

People throw the words *equity*, *diversity*, and *inclusion* around like everyone fully understands their depth. Many don't. What do these words *really* mean? Here is what we mean when we use them:

1. **Equity** is about fairness and equal access to education, employment, and the opportunity to succeed.

2. **Diversity** is about the need to value individual differences. It builds on and flows out of the principle of equity.

3. **Inclusion** is about cultivating full and meaningful engagement of those diverse individuals and groups that have historically been excluded. It follows equity and diversity.

Simply put, we provide equal access, we value difference, and we actively include those who have been left out. That means everyone. No one is to be excluded.

Social media has put immediate pressure on organizations to treat not only their employees but all their stakeholder groups with flawless integrity and justice. This makes it even more important for boards to understand the corporation's social strategy around human rights, protection of vulnerable groups, and transparency around the demographic makeup of staffing, promotion, and compensation within the organization and at the board level.

In a nutshell then, what is social license and how do you get one? Social license is the permission to operate and is granted by the people in the communities you touch. You acquire one by proposing how you plan to engage in social responsibility, social rights, and social justice issues. You spell out your side of the covenant. You are clear on who you are, what you are doing, and how you will behave as a responsible citizen. You engage and consult in meaningful ways. And you treat people equitably by valuing diversity and actively including those who have previously been excluded.

What Stakeholder Groups Should Businesses Have Concern for or Have Covenants With?

Both Canada and the United States have statute law that defines the fiduciary duty of boards to act in the best interests of the corporation. That means if you are a board member, you must be loyal to and act in the best interests of the corporation. The corporation is your beneficiary—your helpless child. Some argue that the corporation is just a legal fiction; it has no intrinsic interests of its own. There is a struggle between shareholder and stakeholder interests when defining the corporation's interests.

In the US and elsewhere in the world, the proponents of this perspective are those who would follow the late Milton Friedman's view of social responsibility. Friedman was a Nobel prize-winning economist from the University of Chicago who famously said, "The only social responsibility a corporation has is to its shareholders—to maximize shareholder value."[43] He persevered through his entire career as a champion and proponent of shareholder governance. Even today in the US, the struggle between shareholder and stakeholder governance continues. The evidence of this is in the business roundtable and the annual letters from Larry Fink to corporations and investors.

As is prone to happen in the US, litigation of the matter ensued with the Revlon case. In 1985 Pantry Pride wanted to buy out Revlon. A takeover process was initially negotiated, but no final decision was made. This led Pantry Pride to initiate a hostile takeover. The board of Revlon responded with a stock repurchase plan that was valued higher than what Pantry Pride had been offering. Then the Board initiated a friendly takeover with a different company. Pantry Pride sued for an injunction against the actions of the Board. Pantry Pride had initially offered Revlon $10 a share above the market value.

Pantry Pride's key argument was that the Board refused to take an offer that would have given their shareholders a premium. The court decided that once the board started negotiating for a friendly takeover, they were acting in their personal interest and welfare. By doing so, they denied the shareholders a premium return on their stocks.

The Delaware court ruled that the board's fiduciary duties narrow to maximize shareholder value if a corporation was in end of life, such as in an insolvency, a change in control, or a bid on the table, etc. This is called the Revlon Duties of a board.

Thus began the argument in Canada. Do we too follow the Revlon Duties? The Bell Canada Enterprises (BCE) case was prompted by the Revlon decision in the US, but in Canada the Supreme Court laid the argument to rest in the famous BCE case on December 19, 2008.

BCE put itself up for sale. It was a sealed bid auction. The board then chose what they felt the best offer was. Unfortunately, the offer substantially hurt the value of bondholders, a specific class of stakeholder. The bondholders of BCE sued the company and its board because they believed it followed Revlon Duties and ignored their interests. They felt the board acted solely in the interests of shareholders by accepting an offer to sell the company and that the sale disadvantaged the debenture/bondholders.

The case made its way to the Supreme Court of Canada. The good news is the Court agreed with the bondholders. It ruled that on the one hand, the bondholders were right—the Revlon Duties do not apply in Canada—and the board owes its fiduciary duty to the corporation and all its stakeholders. In Canada, shareholders do not have primacy even in end of life or, as in this case, in an auction such as this. The bad news for the bondholders though was that the Supreme Court ruled that was exactly what the BCE board did; they had not chosen the bid based on maximizing shareholder value. They took into account the interests of BCE's customers, employees, suppliers, communities, creditors, and shareholders and chose the offer that was best overall for the corporation and all its stakeholders. Unfortunately, it was also the offer that disadvantaged the bondholders. The Court determined that the board had, in fact, weighed their interests in their final decision and made a choice that was reasonable.

The Court also realized that boards are placed in a difficult situation. To help boards in the future, the Court listed the minimum key stakeholders whose interests the board needs to consider in making decisions beyond just the shareholders. They are

1. shareholders;

2. employees;

3. suppliers;

4. creditors;

5. consumers (your customers);

6. governments (public interest); and

7. the environment.

This list of stakeholders goes beyond your own business model to what we call in economics *externalities*. Community and society are not explicitly included in the list handed down from the Court, although they are implied. Depending on your organization and the sector you operate in, you will have other stakeholders. Perhaps for you it is an Indigenous community. If you are a not-for-profit, your stakeholders will include your donors and volunteers as well.

This framework as set out by the Supreme Court of Canada is a great way to begin to think about who your stakeholders are as you consider social license.

As we stated earlier, stakeholders—employees, customers, suppliers, creditors, community—are the soul of any organization. The Supreme Court of Canada clarified in their ruling on the BCE case, at a minimum, which stakeholders you need to consider as core stakeholders. This is a starting point. Your organization may have more stakeholders than what the Supreme Court outlined.

What Are the Social Criteria That Investors Look for When Making Investment Decisions?

The board needs to know what social criteria investors and stakeholders look at. These criteria are centered on how the company treats people. They are not limited to, but they concentrate primarily on,

- employee relations, including EDI;

- working conditions, including in some countries and sectors child labor, slavery, and working environment;

- local communities (these criteria seek explicitly to fund projects or institutions that will serve poor and underserved communities globally);

- health and safety; and

- conflict.

We have talked quite a bit in the previous chapters about how investors measure these ESG criteria.

Social impact measurement is a process of understanding how much social change has occurred and how it can be attributed to an organization's activities. This means you look to measure impacts such as

- employment and unemployment;

- livelihood and wealth;

- education and training;

- skills, knowledge, and competencies of the workforce;

- health and physical well-being;

- mental health and well-being;

- privacy, safety, and security; and

- social inclusion or exclusion, access to services, etc.

These are the types of impact metrics that investors will look at. As a result, these are the types of metrics the board will want to have some line of sight to. Once again, we point you to using your Balanced Scorecard Plus to view and communicate these metrics.

How Are Social License and Related Issues Measured?

Anytime we talk about organizational measures, they will vary significantly by country, industry sector, or company. However, there are some generic measures that are widely used and that we can share. Perhaps a way to look at these is through the lens of your stakeholder groups to find metrics for each. Here are some examples:

- **Shareholders:** A good metric would be total shareholder return. This metric integrates both the increase in the share price value and the dividends that a shareholder receives.

- **Employees:** For employees, the measure that is the most popular and the best is the employee engagement index metric. In other words, what matters is not just a single metric such as employee satisfaction or employee loyalty; it is a series of metrics that are integrated together into an index. It's an excellent metric that integrates elements such as empowerment, reach, the equipping of employees, their alignment with the purpose and values of the organization, the extent to which they feel constructively engaged, etc. It captures aspects of satisfaction and loyalty but in a more fulsome and robust way. Measuring employee engagement is an annual or biannual exercise that an organization undertakes. Typically, an external firm that specializes in employee engagement is hired to measure this for you.

- **Suppliers:** You may have a supplier satisfaction score, which is usually survey-based. Suppliers are asked a series of questions, and each result has a numeric value that is weighted and added together to get to your index. This index is then compared year over year. Another metric here could be the expansion or contraction of the credit facility with your suppliers. Are they giving you everything at net thirty, or are your payment terms dropping below that? Are they wanting payment on or before delivery of services?

- **Creditors:** As with suppliers, there are no standard, readily available metrics for this area. People generally feel that if suppliers keep supplying you and lenders keep lending to you, you are probably treating them all right. But that approach is quite reactive.

  A more proactive approach to measuring the strength of your relationship with your creditors might be to consider your debt rating. Your corporate debt rating is likely the most macro metric you could get, and it is externally set by debt-rating agencies, so it has the benefit of being objective. Chances are, however, if your debt rating is poor, so too is your relationship with your creditors and vice versa.

- **Consumers:** One of the best measures of customer satisfaction is Net Promoter Score (NPS). It is based on one question: how likely are you to recommend our products or services to a friend? The NPS is determined by subtracting the percentage of customers who are detractors from the percentage who are promoters. What is generated is a score between -100 and 100. To calculate the score, you survey customers and see how likely they are on a scale of 0-10 to recommend your business. Then you organize responses into Detractors (0–6), Passives (7–8), and Promoters (9–10). Subtract the percentage of Detractors from the percentage of Promoters to determine your overall NPS.

Given the NPS range of -100 to 100, a positive score or NPS above zero is considered *good*, fifty is considered *excellent*, and above seventy is considered *world-class*. Based on global NPS standards, any score above zero is *good*. A good score means most of your customer base is loyal. For example, Apple's NPS is forty-seven, so pretty good. Few organizations score over fifty. You need a strong response to get above zero. Keep in mind that context is also important to this metric. For example, in the financial services industry, an NPS of fifteen is considered extremely high. With this and other metrics, results should always be contextualized.

The NPS metric is seen as the gold standard because it speaks to sustainability and consumer belief in your product. It is a leading, not a lagging indicator. It is an indicator of future success because you know you have strong support from your customers. The NPS is a good metric for how sustainable your product life cycle is. It is easy to ask, easy to calculate, and easy to understand.

- **Governments (public interest):** This area is a little more difficult to measure, but one qualitative metric could be the extent to and ease with which you receive industry and company-friendly legislative and regulatory changes. In other words, you can track how successful you are in obtaining the regulation you are advocating for with governments of differing jurisdictions. This is at least a good outcome-based measure rather than a simple activity measure.

- **Environment:** In the previous chapter, we talked about metrics here like greenhouse gas, air and water quality, recycling, etc.

If you want a really good example of how boards measure social license, we will point you to Walmart. They publish an annual ESG Report that is quite transparent and specific. They set specific, measurable, attainable, resourced, time-bound (SMART) objectives and report against them. For example, they set EDI targets and then measure and report against their progress. They go further and use external benchmarks, so they have someone other than themselves to compare progress against. Then they go above and beyond by providing an additional comprehensive report on EDI as well.

There are many examples out there. The larger the company, usually the more they disclose, so look to companies in your industry and sector to spur ideas on how you can best measure your social covenant with your stakeholders.

That is a whirlwind look at how to measure social impacts with your stakeholder groups. Our goal was to provide a few examples to get you started. We also wanted to show you how reporting *vis-à-vis* your stakeholder groups could be a helpful way for boards to know where the organization stands in terms of its social covenant.

How Can Boards Understand How Well the Business Supports — or Doesn't Support — the Social Aspects of ESG?

Companies get judged on how well they treat employees and how safe employees are kept. And should the organization fail, this judgment comes not only in the courtroom but in the court of public opinion—a public that includes your employee and customer pool. How well are you nurturing the corporate soul?

With the onset of COVID-19 and the impacts of social media, employee health and safety is a material risk in all sectors, even in industries that have historically had minimal risk in this area.

Boards should understand how the business supports—or doesn't—the social aspects of ESG. How does the business model add or create value? How well does it integrate these social considerations in innovative ways to drive value?

For example, during the COVID-19 global pandemic, innovation was the response of many organizations around the world. Businesses were forced to take a hard look at their business models in light of the new normal and to question everything from where and how people work, to permanent consumer and supplier behaviors, to supply chains and product packaging, to online sales and delivery.

Assessing how your organization is doing in these areas may seem a bit overwhelming for some. A good place to start is with the ESG Pulse Check Assessment at the end of this book. You will find ten questions that can get you started. The bulk of these point you back to your workforce.

For reference we are including those questions here:

1. Does your organization have a comprehensive policy for workplace health and safety that you adhere to?

2. Is your organization committed to human capital development through proactive processes of improving employee performance, capabilities, and resources?

3. Has your organization set aggressive targets for equity, diversity, inclusion, and antibias practices?

4. Has your organization implemented a community investment and relations strategy designed to engage

and build understanding with the communities you impact?

5. Does your organization prioritize social investment initiatives that contribute to improving the quality of life of the communities surrounding its operations?

6. Does your organization identify and act upon actual and potential human rights risks for workers in its operations, supply chains, and the services it uses?

7. Does your organization have a workplace benefits package that shows employees that you are invested in not only their overall health but also their future?

8. Does your organization have a labor relations policy that promotes harmonious labor/management relations, productive work environments, and fair and equitable treatment of employees through the consistent application of collective agreements, labor relations legislation, and workplace policies?

9. Does your organization promote a corporate culture of good health including tobacco-free policies that are combined with tobacco cessation campaigns and referral programs?

10. Does your organization have a work-from-home policy that optimizes the benefits while limiting the risks and sets up your employees to be as successful outside the office as they are in it?

These questions are a pulse check. They touch on just some of the stakeholder groups.

What Questions Should the Board Ask About the Social Aspects of ESG?

Boards need to continually probe management on the validity of the business model as it relates to all things social: social license as it is reflected in social responsibility, social rights, and social justice.

If you are just starting out on your ESG journey with your board, or even if you have long been focused on it and want to step back and relook at your approach, here are few questions your board might ask:

1. How confident are we that we are living up to our social license in our communities? What might we do differently or better?

2. How confident are we that our approach to EDI is appropriate and fulsome? What might we do differently or better?

3. How confident are we that we have the right metrics in place to measure and understand our social impacts?

These three questions cover the broad landscape of social license.

Nurture, Protect, and Renew the Soul of the Organization

We began this chapter with the recognition that people are the soul of the organization—the spirit of the organization—and they must be nurtured, protected, and renewed for the organization to succeed. It is because of the organizational soul we do the hard work of measuring the impacts of the organization on its people—employees and other stakeholders alike—at the board level, the highest level of the corporation.

Our social license, like any license we seek to obtain, must be earned. Earning it requires diligence and perseverance in being socially responsible, respect and support for the social rights of others, and proactivity in our efforts to attain genuine social justice.

CHAPTER 4
HOW THE G OF ESG EMPOWERS YOU TO OUTPERFORM YOUR COMPETITION

If well-governed organizations outperform those that are not, then good governance will give you a competitive advantage. But can we really prove this claim?

Do Better-Governed Organizations Really Outperform Poorly-Governed Ones?

Why do I even pose that question? It is because good governance matters. Well-governed organizations do outperform poorly-governed ones on every important metric. Just like the environment matters and people matter, good governance also matters. Governance is the system that directs and controls how the company treats and respects the environment and its people. Governance closes the circle.

In 1998 David and I conducted research and wrote a report for The Conference Board of Canada, called *Success in the Boardroom*.[44] We created a governance index and tracked about sixty companies against it over twenty-five years of their history.

The index was made up of twenty governance practices that are considered best practices. Practices such as board diversity, board independence, effective board oversight, and functioning, among others. Firstly, at a time when many espoused the belief that governance practices couldn't be measured, we were able to demonstrate that it could be. Secondly, we found clear linkages between successful companies and those that scored highly on the governance index. We uncovered these connections by correlating measures of revenue and profit growth and the scope of operations and recognition of their leadership in their respective industry sectors to the governance index. The results were quite striking.

Since that time, many other researchers have published showing similar linkages. For example, in 2016 Deloitte published a research study claiming, "Our research results support the hypothesis that good governance enhances corporate performance."[45] They identified six good governance variables that they felt contributed to enhanced corporate performance. Theirs was a much smaller list than our twenty-point index, but similar to ours, their list included board independence, board diversity, remuneration, characteristics of the CEO, oversight, and ownership structure.

In 2018 four academic researchers from the Nyenrode Business University in the Netherlands concluded their ten-year study and claimed that their research "provides evidence for the correlation between five corporate governance variables (board independence, board diversity, CEO characteristics, remuneration, and oversight) and company performance."[46] They have very similar markers to ours and the Deloitte study.

These governance variables are proxy indicators. They are what we can readily see, measure, and report against. However, they are but the tip of the iceberg. They are visible indicators of the governance health of the organization.

All three reports make the point that one size won't fit all. The best governance practice is the practice that is best for *your* organization at a given point in its own history. But there are some governance practices that will lead to better performance for all.

There are dozens of similar reports out there. Yet, there are still those few who like to claim that that there is no definitive proof that good governance is linked to good performance. They say no one yet has proven causality.

Why are we telling you about all this research? Here's our point. If good governance doesn't make any difference to corporate performance, why is it that anecdotally we are able to see that well-governed companies do better than those that aren't? And why is it that institutional and large investors, rating agencies, and trust intermediaries, among others, will only recommend or invest in companies that are well-governed?

The answer is that we know it matters. Good governance does make a difference. We have seen the failures and the successes that are linked to either poor or good governance with our own eyes. We have seen it in the 1990s when the Cadbury Report and "Where Were the Directors" were published, both landmark reports linking corporate failures to poor governance. We've seen it in the Enron and WorldCom failures and dozens more like them. More recently, we have seen it in the likes of WE Charity, an organization that had several red governance flags waving, all of which went unnoticed until it was far too late. Of course, good governance matters.

Perhaps the holy grail has not yet been found where one can definitively say, "If you institute these ten governance practices exactly as prescribed, you will have exponential corporate success." Perhaps causality has not yet been clearly demonstrated. Yet, we can say with certainty that from a qualitative, anecdotal perspective, good governance matters; it does add value, and it makes a positive impact on corporate performance.

What Does a Good Governance System Look Like?

That leads us to the question of what a good governance system looks like. Is it more than five or six variables that Deloitte and others have linked to corporate performance?

Does good governance, or do boards for that matter, make any difference to corporate performance, or are they really like parsley on a plate? (They take up space, they look pretty, but they add little nutritional value.) We would argue that boards and governance need to add nutritional value. They need to be much more than parsley on a plate.

Let's begin with the authoritative definition of corporate governance, and then we will describe the governance model that is built on it.

Corporate governance is defined as "the system by which organizations are directed and controlled."[47] This is a clear, helpful, and practical definition that continues to be definitive around the world today, and it becomes the basis for the governance framework. Boards of directors are responsible for the governance of their organizations where there is a separation of ownership and management. The board is vested with the legal power and authority to govern the corporation. This small group of independent-minded individuals is to think and act in the best interest of the corporation. They are responsible for the governance system—for direction and control.

They fulfill their governance duties by focusing on strategic

- direction, i.e., planning, delegation, policy setting, risk management, and resourcing; and

- control, i.e., oversight, monitoring, policy compliance, evaluation, measurement, and reporting.

An effective board concentrates its time and energy on providing strategic direction and control of the organization. The board, as the governing body, sets the direction and uses its controls to ensure the organization is on course. For an organization to be *in control* strategically, the board has confidence and they have gained reasonable assurance that the organization is moving in the direction that it has approved.

The board focuses on governance, the strategic direction, and control, whereas the CEO, along with their executive team and staff, undertakes the actual day-to-day work of the organization and the operational system, where they develop and deliver products and services.

The work of the board and CEO is integrative. They are partners collaborating to articulate and achieve the organization's mission, vision, goals, and objectives. Both do what they are uniquely equipped to do, each respecting the other's potential to succeed and to excel.

A defining feature of an effective governing board is that it draws *a bright line* between its governance roles and responsibilities versus those of the CEO and management team. This separation of duties is central to the board exercising independent oversight and ensuring accountability of the management and staff through the board's one employee, the CEO.

Over our thirty-year history working full-time in corporate governance, we have developed a governance framework that has been adopted around the world and across sectors.

Governance begins with direction. Setting direction is like setting the rudder of the ship, i. e., the corporation. Establishing direction matches the unmet needs of the owners with the best ideas of management.

The framework for direction has five levels:

The 5 Tools for Direction

Strategy Direction	Strategic Plan *Where are we headed?*
Performance & Risk Direction	Risk Appetites & Tolerances *What obstacles and opportunities might we face along the way?*
People Direction	CEO Job Description, Performance Mandate, Board & Committee Charters *Who will do what?*
Policy Direction	Board and Other Governance Related Policies *What are the boundaries and guidelines?*
Resource Direction	Budget, Business Plan *How will we resource our efforts?*

The highest level is *strategy*. The Strategic Plan is the primary tool in direction setting. Everything else in the system hangs from and aligns to this. The strategic direction of the organization answers the questions, "Why are we here?", "Where are we headed?", and "What are the values, vision, mission, and goals of the organization?"

The second level is performance and risk direction. This answers the questions, "What are the obstacles and opportunities we might face along the way?", "What are the specific SMART performance targets that will be set for the organization?", and "What are the risk tolerances and appetites we will attach to those objectives and targets?"

The third level of the governance system is people direction. A large part of this area is ensuring the right CEO is in place and clarifying their expectations and accountabilities. The other part of this area is the board itself: board succession and renewal, how you organize the board and its committees. This third level also includes the setting of compensation for the CEO, the executive, and the board and answers the question, "Who will do what?"

The fourth level is policy direction, which answers the question, "What are the boundaries and guidelines within which we will operate?" The board signs off on a small number of policies which are the red lines, the boundaries, and the rules of the road that management follows between board meetings. It makes clear what the delegated authority and approvals of management are.

The fifth and final level of the governance system is resource direction. It answers the question, "How will we resource our efforts?" Resource direction is largely rolled up into the financial plan—the budget. Even though we have human, material, technical, capital, and other resources, those are all allocated and paid for by the budget. Annually, the board approves the budget that will resource the organization's efforts.

That's direction. That's what we like to call the front end of governance.

Control is the back end.

Remember, control is about gaining reasonable assurance and confidence that the organization is going in the direction that was set. That means control is primarily about monitoring, evaluating, and reporting.

We will describe the five levels of control, this time from the bottom up.

The 5 Tools for Control

Strategy Control	**The Annual Report** *Where are we compared to where we said we would be?*
Performance & Risk Control	**Scorecard, Dashboard, Risk/Heat Map** *How do we measure up & how well have we mitigated risks & acted on opportunities?*
People Control	**Board and CEO Evaluations** *How well did we perform?*
Policy Control	**Policy Compliance, Internal Audit Reports, Minutes** *How effective were our policies and what must be updated or adapted?*
Resource Control	**Interim (Quarterly) Financial Statements** *How are we doing compared to budget?*

The fifth level of control is resource control. This level answers the questions, "How are we doing compared to budget?" and "What is the overall financial health and therefore the general health of the organization?"

The fourth level is policy control, which answers the questions, "How effective are our policies, and what must be updated or adapted?" and "Are we in compliance with approved policies and regulations?" The board will receive reports on compliance with policy, some of which will come from internal audit. The board will test the polices to ensure they are current and effective or to determine if they need updating. This is a large part of the job of the board and occurs largely at the board committee level as well as the resource control level.

The third level is people control. This too usually happens at a board committee level. This level answers the question, "How well are the people doing?" and includes the formal evaluation of the effectiveness of the CEO and the board.

The second level is performance and risk control. This is the level where the board receives reporting against the SMART targets and risk appetites and tolerances that were set in the front-end, directional side of the governance system. That reporting may be in the form of a corporate scorecard, dashboard, risk heat maps, or the like. Such reports are normally received by the board on a quarterly basis. These reports are intended to answer the questions, "How do we measure up?" and "How well have we mitigated our risks and acted on our opportunities?"

Finally, there is a roll up to strategy in our first level. Everything from the lower levels gets rolled up on an annual basis. This level answers the questions, "Where are we compared to where we said we would be?", "How are we doing compared to our strategic plan and corporate objectives?", "How are we doing in terms of the financial health of the organization, as validated through an external auditor?", "How are we doing in compensation as disclosed in a Compensation Discussion and Analysis Report?", and "How are we doing in ESG as confirmed through an ESG Disclosure Report?" Often the answers to these questions are rolled up and combined into a single annual report, which is publicly disclosed. This level becomes the primary accountability mechanism for the organization to its owners and other stakeholders.

When we put this all together, we have five levels of direction and five levels of control. The control tools inform each level of direction. In other words, you receive actual results in terms of how you are doing in each of the five levels. They should all integrate and align. Everything should have line of sight back to the strategic direction, the long-term vision, and mission of the organization.

Together the governance system looks something like this:

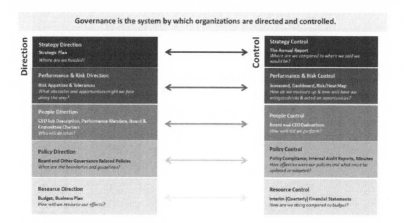

Governance is the system by which organizations are directed and controlled.

Boards fulfill their governance roles and responsibilities by ensuring that these ten key governance documents/tools are in place and that they are aligned vertically and horizontally.

This framework is the essence of the value proposition that a board brings to governance. If a board is not adding value to these five levels of governance using these ten tools, then arguably it may be just like parsley on a plate—adding little nutritional value.

What is our point here? It doesn't really matter if you can identify exactly which good governance practices you can quantifiably link to improved corporate performance. Proving causality isn't the point. Good governance, not in its parts but as a whole, is a necessary ingredient to enhanced corporate performance.

If you only do those five aspects of governance that are proven to link to strong corporate performance, would the governance system work well and add value? We suspect not. Is having an independent and diverse board that aligns the compensation of a great CEO with the ownership structure of the organization enough? It is a great start, but we suspect this would leave significant holes in the governance system.

For example, remove oversight of the financial system from the governance system. Decide that the board no longer needs to approve the budget and receive quarterly financial reports. Or decide that there is no need for ensuring clarity of the role of the board or CEO, and remove people direction. Remove the process of evaluation and assessment. Or perhaps just stop approving a strategic plan and assessing risk in any systematic way. What about reporting, compliance, and transparency? You cannot just remove these integrated pieces from the governance system and reduce it solely to what can be quantifiably measured.

Governance is a system by which organizations are directed and controlled. You cannot cherry-pick the parts of the systems that you like or don't like. You need the whole system. In governance there are some best practices, some good practices, and some bad practices. You have choices in governance, but you cannot throw away the fundamental pieces of the governance system. It really is a system.

What Governance Criteria Do Investors, Donors, and Other Stakeholders Look for Before Making Decisions About Investing Their Time and Money into the Organization?

There are striking similarities between what investors, donors, and other stakeholders look for in making investment decisions and the handful of metrics researchers tell us link to corporate performance.

Here are some facts reported by the Institute of Internal Auditors out of Australia recently:

More than 80% of mainstream investors now consider ESG information when making investment decisions. There are currently $23 trillion of assets being professionally managed under responsible investment strategies, an increase of 25% since 2014 which exceeds the gross domestic product of the entire USA economy.[48]

Most individual (retail) investors rely on what we call *trust intermediaries* to evaluate and report on the governance of corporations, to help them make their investment decisions. Single investors don't have the resources to investigate individual corporations. They rely on other organizations to do that on their behalf. These organizations are called trust intermediaries because as we trust the intermediary, we therefore trust the organization they have evaluated. This is an important principle in trust and in good governance.

In the for-profit sector, when we talk about investments of capital in the public market, the key trust intermediaries are proxy advisory firms. There are a small number of global proxy advisory firms, for example Glass Lewis & Co., who are trust intermediaries that investment firms pay to review and rate the governance of firms that issue capital in public markets. These proxy advisory firms research companies and provide investment and voting advice to investors based on their findings. They play a powerful role in the investment world.

Not all their information is publicly available; however, many of them do publish their ratings. The Globe and Mail's *Board Games* is a good example of one such publication. In this case, a media firm rates every publicly traded firm in Canada against their own set of criteria for good governance. These criteria go well beyond the handful of metrics discussed earlier. Each year the media firm publishes their complete findings in what they call their *Board Games* for everyone to see and use. This year will be their twentieth year doing this.

The publication of ratings has a powerful influence on governance practices. The CEOs and CIOs of the biggest corporations in the country await with some trepidation the publication of *Board Games*. Receiving a high rating can make conversations with investors much easier, but a lower rating can deflate a company's share price and lead to internal governance reviews and changes.

As an example, we at Governance Solutions had a company engage us to help them get higher rankings in the Globe and Mail's *Board Games*. They had two different drivers for this. One was that they were embarrassed that they kept getting low ratings. The second was more pragmatic. Their largest investor had threatened to pull their investment and end their relationship if they didn't solve the problem by the next edition. Their investor was most concerned about board diversity and gave the company a year to transform the diversity profile of their board and significantly improve their ratings. You cannot underestimate the impact of external intermediaries.

Trust intermediaries exist in sectors beyond for-profit share corporations. In the faith-based charity sector in the US, The Evangelical Council for Financial Accountability (ECFA) certification is considered a *passport* needed before donors will give to a charity in this sector. If the ECFA withdraws its certification, donor funds will dry up. The Canadian equivalent is the Canadian Centre for Christian Charities (CCCC). The accreditation of the CCCC provides donors with confidence of a charity's credibility.

Similarly, in the health sector in Canada, Accreditation Canada evaluates the governance practices of hospitals and health centers, issuing certifications which are widely respected as *seals of approval* of good governance. The public and governments would demand changes if a hospital failed to achieve this certification.

These are just some examples of trust intermediaries— those organizations that do the homework for you. You trust in their work and therefore by extension you trust the organizations to the level they suggest.

Typically investors and stakeholders examine governance criteria around how a corporation polices and governs itself. Their main focus is on looking for

- transparency in reporting—including tax strategy;

- executive compensation alignment;

- donations and political lobbying involvement;

- signs of corruption and bribery; and

- board diversity, independence, and ownership structure.

These are just the primary aspects of governance they look for.

You can see some commonalities in what the large investors look for. The quantifiable metrics have been linked to corporate performance—practices such as executive compensation, diversity, independence, and ownership structure. But good governance practices go beyond those quantifiable aspects of governance to transparency, ethics, and beyond.

There is a slew of governance markers that interested parties want to know about here. Interest extends to regulatory compliance, risk management, conflicts of interest, anticompetitive behavior, and whistle-blower policies. In other words, it's good governance.

A great example here is board diversity. There is active pressure for enhanced diversity in organizations—on their leadership teams and in their boardrooms. We have long been advocates for board diversity, publishing our first report on this in 2002.[49] We are advocates not only because embracing diversification is the right thing to do societally but because the research clearly shows that doing so enhances and improves governance performance.

Governments are getting into the legislative game when it comes to diversity. Since the early 2000s, we have seen gender diversity quotas in some European countries when it comes to board seats. For example, Norway, Spain, and France have all instituted diversity quotas. In 2020 California passed a bill requiring boardrooms to be more racially diverse. This bill adds to their 2018 legislation requiring gender diversity on boards. While California was an early adopter of regulating boardroom diversity, other governments have followed and will continue to follow suit.

As an interesting aside, in the 2016 and 2018 report we quoted earlier, researchers found that diversity no longer correlates as contributing to stronger results when it is mandated. *Both/and* is needed—*both* competent *and* diverse board members are the keys to success here. Diversity for the sake of diversity is not the goal. The goal is to build diversity while bringing competent people into the boardroom. This finding points to the risk of government overreach having unintended consequence.

The point here is that you need to have competent people in the boardroom. Good governance is not just about structure and process. In fact, we would say good governance goes beyond the governance system to board-room dynamics and culture.

We would not be surprised to see in the not-too-distant future that investors and their proxies are looking for a metric that will assess the health of boardroom culture. We say that because we are seeing early evidence of this.

In 2017 the National Association of Corporate Directors (NACD) in the US published a report called *Culture as a Corporate Asset* in which they made ten recommendations on the role of the board in culture. One of those recommendations was that directors should review the culture of the whole board and its key committees on a regular basis, both formally (via the evaluation process) and informally (by making time for reflective conversation in executive sessions). The results of these reviews should inform board composition, succession planning especially for leadership roles on the board and continuous improvement efforts in board operating processes.[50]

It may take some time, but we believe that boardroom culture will be another metric that will become a more formal part of the ESG reporting framework. You can have the world's best governance structure, but if people don't behave in the boardroom, and its culture is dysfunctional, then your great governance structure and system get significantly weakened.

What the NACD did not do was provide guidance on how to measure boardroom culture. The good news is we at Governance Solutions have spent years developing tools for this! As a reader of this book, you can gain free access to a couple of them, which you can use to test for two things: culture type and cultural health. One tool will allow you to determine what type of boardroom culture you have and therefore what to watch out for.[51] The other will tell you how healthy your boardroom culture is.[52]

How Can We Measure Our Governance and All Our ESG Efforts Using a Simple, Single Tool?

In previous chapters we have talked about a *balanced scorecard* as a strategic planning framework initially developed by Kaplan and Norton out of Harvard Business School. It was developed in the early 1990s as an attempt to help firms measure business performance using both financial and nonfinancial data. Kaplan and Norton were faced with the challenge that no two organizations have the same strategic plan. Every organization has a different vision, mission, values, goals, objectives, and strategies. Each has a differing environmental scan and risk profile, which are ever changing. Kaplan and Norton needed a tool that would help any organization with strategic planning.

That is when they came up with the concept of a balanced scorecard to help organizations plan, measure, and integrate financial and nonfinancial performance. Their stated aim of the balanced scorecard was "to align business activities to the vision and strategy of the organization, improve internal and external communications, and monitor organization performance against strategic goals."[53]

Kaplan and Norton recognized that no single measures could give a broad picture of the organization's health. Stock price alone is not a good enough proxy; it has far too many variables included in it. So instead of a single measure they thought, why not a use a composite scorecard involving several different measures—a balanced set of measures: financial, client/customer, process, and learning and growth. These four areas are common to any organization in any sector in any country. The framework allows any organization to select critical measures for each of these four perspectives. In this way a management team, board, or outside observer can get a balanced view of the overall health of the organization.

These four perspectives, or dimensions, link together in a value chain.

Balanced Scorecard Value Chain in For-Profit Organizations

If you are a for-profit organization, the value chain begins with *learning and growth*. That is the input level of the value chain. This means that the first dimension of the scorecard you want to measure is the people side of the organization. You will want to know how effectively you are attracting, retaining, motivating, and engaging the human resources of the organization. The purpose of this dimension is to ensure you effectively manage talent to ensure a highly motivated, well-trained, and engaged workforce.

The second dimension of a balanced scorecard is *process*. This dimension looks at the quality process that the human resources of the organization will use to create the organization's products and services. Sometimes this layer is called *quality*.

The next dimension is called *client* or *customer*. Now that we have produced these products and services, what do our customers think of them? How do they use our products and services? To what extent do they value them?

The financial dimension is at the pinnacle of the balanced scorecard. That is, how are we doing *financially* in term of the sales of our products and services? Do we hold a good share of the market? What are our revenues, margins, and profits? Are we growing financially, and how is our growth contributing to shareholder value?

The not-for-profit and public sectors use the same four dimensions; they are just in a different order.

Balanced Scorecard Value Chain in Not-for-profit and Public Sector Organizations

Financial feeds the value chain. We look for donors and funders as a means toward an end. The financial resources are used to hire people who can engage in quality processes producing and distributing products and services to our client, who is the pinnacle of the balanced scorecard in those sectors.

That is the traditional balanced scorecard.

Over the years, we recognized that the four dimensions alone left some gaps. Truly great companies need and want to measure another dimension, which is ESG. These (ESG) elements of corporate life and performance are not adequately captured in the original, traditional, Kaplan and Norton model, or if they are, they are forced into it.

Adding a fifth dimension for ESG has always made sense to us.

Over our years of doing strategic planning, conducting research, and consulting with hundreds of organizations and their boards, we added this fifth dimension to the balance scorecard and recommend using what we call a Balanced Scorecard Plus. The *plus* takes ESG into account and gives stakeholders a more fulsome view of what success looks like.

Balanced Scorecard Plus©: The Value Chain

For the board, this means approving high-level goals and related performance measures in each of the five areas of the Balanced Scorecard Plus: financial, client/customer, process, learning and growth, and our added fifth dimension, ESG. Each goal area is then supported by a suite of SMART objectives.

In their direction setting role, boards approve an overarching goal and performance measures in each of these dimensions. In their control role, the board gains reasonable assurance that the organization is on track by approving, receiving, monitoring, and evaluating performance metrics as well as risk appetites and tolerances for each dimension. Boards follow progress on these through a board-level scorecard.

This is a way of integrating ESG seamlessly into your balanced scorecard and therefore your board reporting.

Sometimes people look at the Balanced Scorecard Plus and dismiss it as somewhat of a simple tool, but the greatest benefit of this tool is its simplicity.

We met with a board recently that was having challenges getting a clear, balanced line of sight to the organization's various parts. They were using a combination of several processes (e. g. Six Sigma, LEAN, the 12 Week Year, swim lanes, and at least four other processes) in their efforts to gain a clear line of sight into and alignment of the organization's efforts.

Like many organizations, they jumped on the latest and greatest concept or book someone had read and were trying to paste these individual processes all into an integrated whole. It wasn't working. Simplifying to a clean Balanced Scorecard Plus with SMART objectives enabled them to bring all these disparate themes and processes together into a single, clear system.

Don't add ESG as a new, complex system off to the side. Make it an integral part of your Balanced Scorecard Plus system.

How Do Boards Oversee ESG? Is It Time for Boards to Strike ESG Committees or Not?

This is a frequently asked question we get: should the board strike an ESG Committee?

The short answer is no. No, you do not need yet another board committee! There are some boards that have done this. There are also some boards that have assigned ESG oversight to an existing standing committee. Others have renamed the Governance Committee to the ESG Committee to reflect an expanded scope. We do not believe this is the direction to go. Here's why.

ESG cuts across the organization. It cuts across human resources. It cuts across governance. It cuts across the financial system. It cuts across the enterprise-wide risk system. And it impacts innovation, reputation, and operationalization. It is broad. Like the roll up of the balanced scorecard in financial, customer, process, and learning and growth, ESG is a board-level oversight dimension.

In those organizations that have struck an ESG Committee we see two problems occur:

1. Overlaps and gaps develop between committees, causing confusion and duplication of effort. For example, an overlap in the direction and control of health and safety could be duplicated between an ESG Committee and the Human Resources Committee. The lines between committees subsequently blur, causing confusion, stress, and strain between them.

2. The committee becomes operational, quickly violating the board/management line. Not only do they get scope creep in the other committees, they also get scope creep into operations. Much of ESG is operational, but all the board really needs to see are the high-level aspects of ESG.

This is a little like the debate about whether to have a subcommittee of the board for risk. Some organizations have chosen to have one. Others delegate risk to the Audit and Finance Committee. Still others parcel pieces of risk out to other various committees. For example, human resources risk is assigned to the Human Resources Committee, financial risk to the Audit and Finance Committee, and governance risk to the Governance Committee.

There are some organizations in certain sectors that may need a risk committee; however, the vast majority do not. Risks intersect and crosscut each other—one risk impacts and interrelates with another or even ten others and together, risk is enterprise-wide. This means risk is usually best overseen by the board itself.

When we think about ESG, for example, some of the governance considerations and programs within ESG would naturally fit with the Governance and Nominations Committee. Social could easily fit with HR. But environment is not a natural fit for Audit and Finance or either of the other core board committees.

So while there may be specific risks or pieces of ESG that may be explicitly assigned to a committee for diligence work, the natural landing spot for this enterprise-wide, crosscutting set of measurement criteria we call ESG is the board itself.

At the end of the day, each board will need to decide how it will ensure line of sight on ESG to itself and to its various stakeholders. The Governance Committee could be well suited to ensure ESG reporting outwardly to stakeholders; however, oversight of the area is a higher-level activity. We suggest you make ESG part of your Balanced Scorecard Plus. That way the entire board gets line of sight and performance reporting against it. We encourage you to resist the temptation to strike yet another board committee that would no doubt put pressure on the bright red line between where management's job ends and where the board's begins.

What Are Some Questions the Board Can Be Asking About the G of ESG?

We end this chapter, as we have the others, with a handful of questions the board can be asking to get started on the G of the ESG journey:

1. To what extent is our board independent and free from conflicts of interest, as well as political and other forms of interference?

2. How defensible and aligned is our executive compensation philosophy and strategy?

3. Do we have a diversity strategy with meaningful targets for the board and management? If not, why not?

4. How good is our governance really?

5. Does our organization produce a publicly available annual report detailing its ESG performance and results of ESG performance measures? If not, will we? If yes, is it transparent and robust enough?

In terms of assessing where your organization is at, addressing these questions may seem a bit overwhelming for some. To help, this is another reminder that you can start with the ESG Pulse Check Assessment at the end of this book (Appendix 1). The third section of that assessment is related to governance, and we would urge you to complete that assessment and see how your board measures up.

For reference, those questions are provided here:

1. Does your board adopt and excel in good corporate governance practices?

2. Does your organization's board meet or exceed expectations for independence from management?

3. Does your board approve and monitor a Conflict of Interest Policy and process that ensures the highest public confidence in the integrity of the organization and its people?

4. Does your board approve and monitor a Business Conduct and Ethics Policy that deters wrongdoing, promotes honest and ethical conduct, and ensures business is conducted in a consistently legal and ethical manner?

5. Does your board approve and monitor a Transparency and Disclosure Policy that, while protecting legitimately confidential business information, supports transparent disclosure to the public, investors, employees, customers, creditors, and other relevant parties in a timely, accurate, complete, understandable, convenient, and affordable manner?

6. Does your board approve and monitor a policy that prohibits the organization from making corporate political contributions?

7. Does your board ensure direct alignment of executive compensation to corporate results and ESG metrics and ensure full disclosure of board and executive compensation?

8. Does your board set aggressive targets for diversity and inclusion in the boardroom and c-suite?

9. Has your board approved an anticorruption policy setting a zero-tolerance approach to bribery and corruption?

10. Does your board assess its own culture using a third party on at least a biannual basis?

Governance Closes the Circle

Once upon a time, there was a company that lost millions of dollars. The CEO was the king of this company, and everyone bowed to his every whim. His edicts were observed, his excuses accepted, and his failings overlooked. The board of directors would not dare challenge the king's proclamations.

Then one day, a new board member was elected to join the group of fearful leaders. This new board member was different from the rest. She was not afraid. She was independently minded. She was a Professional Director.[54] She understood her role. She understood governance, what it meant to be a well-governed company, and how to get there.

Together, the burning platform of financial losses and the perseverance of one brave soul began to turn the tide and restore the kingdom. It wasn't long before the king began to listen to the voice of reason. He too learned where to draw the governance lines and how good governance would help turn the company around.

This *once-upon-a-time* story is a true one. In our consulting practice, we see this type of situation every day. We see CEOs try to run the governance system while board members try to run the operational system. This role confusion is but a symptom of disrespect for and a lack of role clarity about the line between the two systems. When the board, CEOs, and executives do not understand their role in governance, they fail to recognize and harness the power of good governance. Everyone in the kingdom suffers for it.

We will say it again: good governance matters. It just does. Well-governed organizations do outperform poorly-governed ones. Just like the environment matters and people matter, good governance matters. Governance is the system that directs and controls how the company treats and respects the environment and its people. Governance closes the circle.

AFTERWORD

Do more! Wherever you are on your own ESG journey, there will always be more you can do. The more you do, the more you, the environment, your organization, stakeholders, and owners will benefit. ESG really is win-win-win!

You can protect and renew the environment and save money at the same time. You can have, and support, justice and profit at the same time. You can invest in good governance and get a return on that investment at the same time.

Together we can quiet the screams of our planet, people, and organizations and traverse the raging river of ESG. As our world emerges from the COVID-19 crisis and governments and corporations continue to focus on environmental and current social justice movements, we are convinced that our corporate lives and social covenant will be changed forever. That change will be for the good in terms of our care for stakeholders and long-term sustainability. And focusing on ESG will push us ever closer to being the best corporate citizens we can be.

No one large corporation doing everything they need to do will be able to change the trajectory of the damage that humanity has inflicted on our natural environment, but together, all of us can.

Our social license, like any license we seek to obtain, must be earned. Earning it requires diligence and perseverance in being socially responsible, respectful, and supportive for the social rights of others and proactivity in our efforts to attain genuine social justice.

The natural environment, the people who live in it, and the organizations they serve and work in matter. How we treat them will be our one true legacy.

What Are Your Next Steps Related to ESG in Your Organization?

1. Where are you going to focus your next ESG steps?

    a. environment

    b. social

    c. governance

    d. all of the above

    e. I am not planning on taking any next steps

2. What will those next steps be?

    a. planning

    b. implementation

    c. reporting

    d. measuring

e. monitoring

f. all of the above

3. Why will you be taking those steps?

a. I have learned a new way of looking at these issues.

b. It is just a natural progression of what we are already doing.

c. I believe it will improve the value of our organization.

d. I want to satisfy external stakeholders or agencies.

e. all of the above

APPENDIX 1
ESG PULSE CHECK ASSESSMENT FOR BOARDS

Answer *yes* or *no* to each of the following questions:

Questions: Environment	Yes/No
1. Your board receives metrics on the organization's contribution to climate change.	Yes ☐ No ☐ N/A ☐
2. Your organization has a proactive antipollution and waste management policy.	Yes ☐ No ☐ N/A ☐
3. Your organization uses and invests in green technology in meaningful ways.	Yes ☐ No ☐ N/A ☐
4. Your organization replenishes energy at a rate that is equal to or faster than the rate at which it is consumed.	Yes ☐ No ☐ N/A ☐
5. Your organization is housed in green buildings and facilities.	Yes ☐ No ☐ N/A ☐

6. Your organization has a target to have a carbon neutral footprint and is actively pursuing it.	Yes ☐ No ☐ N/A ☐
7. Your organization handles hazardous waste in a way that it is collected, stored, transported, treated, recovered, and disposed of to reduce adverse effects to human health and the environment.	Yes ☐ No ☐ N/A ☐
8. Your organization has a policy for its use of water with an aim toward conservation.	Yes ☐ No ☐ N/A ☐
9. Your organization does everything it can to avoid resource depletion.	Yes ☐ No ☐ N/A ☐
10. Your organization has a policy to use recycled or reused materials as a first and best choice option.	Yes ☐ No ☐ N/A ☐

Count your *yeses* to find out the ESG Score in your boardroom:

E Score

0–4 You have a lagging E score and should create a plan to take your next best steps to protect the environment at your earliest opportunity.

5–7 You have an average E score and should prioritize and take the next steps in your journey to protect the environment.

8–10 You have a leading E score and should be proud of your organization—keep up the good work and share your story with others!

Questions: Social	*Yes/No*
1. Your organization has a comprehensive policy for workplace health and safety, which you adhere to.	Yes ☐ No ☐ N/A ☐

2. Your organization is committed to human capital development through proactive processes of improving employee performance, capabilities, and resources.

Yes ☐ No ☐ N/A ☐

3. Your organization has set aggressive targets for equity, diversity, inclusion, and antibias practices.

Yes ☐ No ☐ N/A ☐

4. Your organization implements a community investment and relations strategy designed to engage and build understanding with the communities impacted by it.

Yes ☐ No ☐ N/A ☐

5. Your organization prioritizes social investment initiatives that contribute to improving the quality of life of the communities surrounding its operations and continues to make impacts beyond its initial participation.

Yes ☐ No ☐ N/A ☐

6. Your organization identifies and acts upon actual and potential human rights risks for workers in its operations, supply chains, and the services it uses.

Yes ☐ No ☐ N/A ☐

7. Your organization has a workplace benefits package that shows employees that you are invested in not only their overall health but also their future.

Yes ☐ No ☐ N/A ☐

8. Your organization has a labor relations policy that promotes harmonious labor/management relations, productive work environments, and fair and equitable treatment of employees through the consistent application of collective agreements, labor relations legislation, and workplace policies.

Yes ☐ No ☐ N/A ☐

9. Your organization promotes a corporate culture of good health including tobacco-free policies that are combined with tobacco cessation campaigns and referral programs.

Yes ☐ No ☐ N/A ☐

10. Your organization has a work-from-home policy that optimizes the benefits while limiting the risks and sets up your employees to be as successful outside the office as they are in it.

Yes ☐ No ☐ N/A ☐

S Score

0–4 You have a low S score and should create a plan to take your next best steps to earning your social license at your earliest opportunity.

5–8 You have a moderate S score and should prioritize and take the next steps in your journey to securing your social license to operate.

8–10 You have a high S score and should be proud of your organization—keep up the good work and share your story with others!

Questions: Governance	Yes/No
1. Your board adopts and excels in good corporate governance practices.	Yes ☐ No ☐ N/A ☐
2. Your board meets or exceeds expectations for independence from management.	Yes ☐ No ☐ N/A ☐
3. Your board approves and monitors a Conflict of Interest Policy and process that ensures the highest public confidence in the integrity of the organization and its people.	Yes ☐ No ☐ N/A ☐
4. Your board approves and monitors a Business Conduct and Ethics Policy that deters wrongdoing, promotes honest and ethical conduct, and ensures business is conducted in a consistently legal and ethical manner.	Yes ☐ No ☐ N/A ☐
5. Your board approves and monitors a Transparency and Disclosure Policy that, while protecting legitimately confidential business information, supports transparent disclosure to the public, investors, employees, customers, creditors, and other relevant parties in a timely, accurate, complete, understandable, convenient, and affordable manner.	Yes ☐ No ☐ N/A ☐

6. Your board approves and monitors a policy that prohibits the organization from making corporate political contributions.	Yes ☐ No ☐ N/A ☐
7. Your board ensures direct alignment of executive compensation to corporate results and ESG metrics and ensures full disclosure of board and executive compensation.	Yes ☐ No ☐ N/A ☐
8. Your board sets aggressive targets for diversity and inclusion in the boardroom and c-suite.	Yes ☐ No ☐ N/A ☐
9. Your board has approved an anticorruption policy setting a zero-tolerance approach to bribery and corruption.	Yes ☐ No ☐ N/A ☐
10. Your board assesses its own culture using a third party on at least a biannual basis.	Yes ☐ No ☐ N/A ☐

G Score

0–4 You have a low G score and should create a plan to take your next best steps to improve your governance at your earliest opportunity.

5–8 You have a moderate G score and should prioritize and take the next steps in your good governance journey.

8–10 You have a high G score and should be proud of your organization—keep up the good work and share your story with others!

Your ESG Score

Your E Score (Environment)	
Your S Score (Social)	
Your G Score (Governance)	
Your Total ESG Score	

APPENDIX 2
ESG GUIDELINES AND ACCEPTED PROTOCOLS

- Global Reporting Initiative (GRI): globalreporting.org
- AccountAbility: accountability.org
- Greenhouse Gas Protocol (GHG): ghgprotocol.org
- UN Sustainability Goals: sdgs.un.org/goals
- The Global Carbon Project (GCP): globalcarbonproject.org/
- Carbon Disclosure Project (CDP): cdp.net
- MSCI: msci.com
- Sustainalytics: sustainalytics.com/
- Retailer Report Card: retailerreportcard.com/

APPENDIX 3
QUESTIONS THE BOARD SHOULD ASK ABOUT ESG

Here are some questions that you can be asking as a board member or executive.

ESG

1. How confident are we that we have a fully integrated and financially material ESG program?

2. Does the organization produce a publicly available annual report detailing its ESG performance and results of ESG performance measures? If not, will we? If yes, how transparent and robust is our ESG reporting and disclosure?

3. How will we evaluate options for enhancing the materiality of our ESG program?

Environment

4. How confident are we that we have implemented environmentally friendly programs?

5. Are we complaint with all environmental regulations?

6. Have we set targets related to our environmental programs, and are we reviewing results against these at the board level?

Social

7. How confident are we that we are living up to our social license in our communities? What might we do differently or better?

8. How confident are we that our approach to EDI is appropriate and fulsome? What might we do differently or better?

9. How confident are we that we have the right metrics in place to measure and understand our social impacts?

Governance

10. To what extent is our board independent and free from conflicts of interest—political and other forms of interference?

11. How defensible and aligned are our executive compensation philosophy and strategy?

12. Do we have a diversity strategy with meaningful targets for the board and management? If not, why not?

13. How good is our governance really?

14. Does the organization produce a publicly available annual report detailing its ESG performance and results of ESG performance measures? If not, will we? If yes, is it transparent and robust enough?

ABOUT THE AUTHORS

Dr. Debra L. Brown

Debra was five years old when her father sat her behind the wheel of the family tractor, pointed at a tree across the field, and told her to drive straight at it, never taking her eye off the mark. It was her first lesson in vision and strategy: know where you're going, and how to get there and stay focused. Today she is a globally respected thought leader and the founder, President, and CEO of Governance Solutions (GSI).

Under Debra's leadership, GSI developed a comprehensive, principles-based governance system that has been adopted by organizations, governments, and not-for-profits around the world. It was also the foundation for The Professional Director Education and Certification Program®.

Prior to founding Governance Solutions, Debra twice served as a CEO and sat on the board of several organizations, including as Board Chair and Governance Committee

Chair. As a result, she is uniquely qualified as a governance advisor with the ability to see issues from both sides of the boardroom table.

Debra has authored dozens of articles and publications, and her books include *Governance Solutions: The Ultimate Guide to Competence and Confidence in the Boardroom*; *Governing in Scary Times: The Board's Roadmap for Governing Through and Beyond an Emergency*; and *Virtually There: Dos and Don'ts for Planning, Chairing, and Holding Virtual Board and Annual General Meetings*. She also writes a column for the Financial Gazette and is a contributing author for Ethical Boardroom Magazine.

Equally prolific outside work, Debra is an enthusiastic painter, poet, and musician. A member of The Institute of Corporate Directors, Debra holds a Doctor of Ministry and a Master of Divinity from Gordon-Conwell Theological Seminary, where she graduated *magna cum laude*.

David A. H. Brown

The son of two bankers, David grew up listening to discussions around the dining room table about business problems—and how to solve them. It's been his passion ever since. Today David is Canada's leading thinker, speaker, writer, and practitioner in corporate governance.

As GSI's Executive Vice-President and the team's lead consultant, David has helped countless organizations improve their governance and board effectiveness. He cares deeply about corporations and their innate capacity to do good as well as their inherent risk of doing bad. His life's work is helping leaders make better choices for themselves and everyone they touch.

Prior to joining Governance Solutions in 1995, David had a distinguished twenty-year career in Canada's financial services industry. As an insolvency specialist, he learned hard lessons about the necessity for good corporate governance—and how badly things can go in its absence.

David holds a Bachelor of Commerce (Hons) from Queen's University in addition to Chartered Director and Professional Director designations in corporate governance. He's also served as an accredited faculty member of several universities, including McMaster University and the Universities of St. Michael's College, Toronto, and Saskatchewan.

ABOUT GOVERNANCE SOLUTIONS

As globally respected leaders in all things governance, we help boards and executives understand their role in governance so they can succeed and their organization can win. Unlock the full potential of your board and governance system and optimize your governance through our superior, integrated portfolio of products and services.

governancesolutions.ca

OTHER BOOKS BY THE AUTHORS

Governance Solutions: The Ultimate Guide to Competence and Confidence in the Boardroom

Today's board members need more tools, not more rules!

Governance Solutions: The Ultimate Guide to Competence and Confidence in the Boardroom is chock-full of governance tools that make the complex seem simple and bring order to the chaos.

This is not just a book *about governance*, it tells you how to *do governance*. Authors David A. H. Brown and Dr. Debra L. Brown deliver

- Proven governance solutions: this book is a single source—the ultimate guide—for solving your governance problems.
- Access: *Governance Solutions* includes almost seventy governance concepts and tools that are unique only to this book.
- Competence and confidence: the book covers the broad spectrum of governance issues from governance structure and process through boardroom leadership, culture, and behavior.
- Answers! This book tells you not only what works but just as importantly, what does not work in governance.

With so many spotlights trained on corporate boards, there could hardly be a better moment for hands-on, cutting-edge guidance on how directors can power success—and avoid traps. David and Debra Brown are world-class experts; their new book earns a place on director desks everywhere.

Stephen Davis, PhD
Associate Director and Senior Fellow
Harvard Law School Programs on Corporate Governance and Institutional Investors

Governing in Scary Times: The Board's Roadmap for Governing Through and Beyond an Emergency

COVID-19 threw the world into scary times!

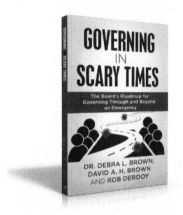

If the global pandemic taught us anything, it's that all organizations need a strategy to manage in a crisis. In *Governing in Scary Times*, authors Dr. Debra L. Brown, David A. H. Brown, and Rob DeRooy offer a step-by-step plan to prepare your board to provide direction for your company and reinforce your stakeholder confidence.

With a combined seventy-five years of experience governing companies and boards, the authors guide you through a process that will prepare you to answer key questions:

- Where are we headed?
- What obstacles and opportunities might we face along the way?
- Who will do what?
- What are the boundaries and guidelines?
- How will we resource our efforts?

Governing in Scary Times is your boardroom roadmap to navigating extreme challenges in your business. From developing a strategic plan to assessing risks and policies to getting and keeping the right people in place, the authors provide practical and proven advice that will equip your company to survive scary times—and come out stronger on the other side.

Another crisis is (always) coming. Use the strategies in *Governing in Scary Times* to ensure your organization is prepared.

The World Went Virtual.
Are you Equipped to
Leverage this Opportunity?

Authors Dr. Debra L. Brown, Rob DeRooy, and Jake Skinner draw from their years of governance and technical experience to share best practices for strengthening unity and community within your organization.

Discover how to optimize your virtual meetings by . . .

- Creating healthy engagement and spirited communication to resolve issues.
- Drawing out people who tend to hold back and quelling others who tend to dominate so all feel heard and respected.
- Establishing agreed upon guidelines that foster progress and growth.

Start tapping into greater levels of success, regardless of where you meet.

Available wherever books are sold.

OPTIMIZE YOUR GOVERNANCE

Propel and optimize your governance effectiveness and get superior corporate results with *Governance Consulting and Coaching.*

Experience clear outcomes, objective assessment, helpful advice, and actionable strategies with our team of consultants who can be trusted to be discreet, sensitive, and practical.

Choose from the following services:

- Comprehensive governance review
- One-on-one coaching in governance skills
- Team coaching to enhance board solidarity
- Help with that difficult director

Schedule an Appointment Today
GovernanceSolutions.ca

UNLEASH YOUR
BOARD'S POTENTIAL

BoardConnex® makes it easy for board members to collaborate securely—anywhere, anytime—using state-of-the-art board portal technology.

BoardConnex is a secure, web-based portal solution that . . .

- Protects sensitive information; worry-free with secure remote access.
- Makes it easy for board members to stay connected and effective at home, the office, and on the go.
- Eliminates paper waste and helps you manage agendas, board packages, and more in less time.
- Empowers your board to make quick, critical decisions based on rapidly emerging opportunity, uncertainty, and risk—any time of day or night, anywhere in the world.
- Simplifies and streamlines the work of your board secretariate. The easy-to-use interface will have you up and running in no time.

Schedule a demonstration today and discover how BoardConnex can transform the way your board engages and collaborates.

Book Your Demo
BoardConnex.com

EARN YOUR PROFESSIONAL DIRECTOR® DESIGNATION

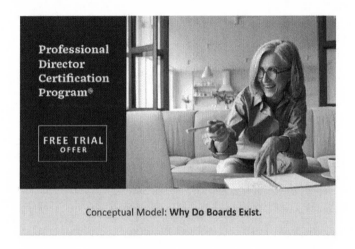

Professional
Director
Certification
Program®

FREE TRIAL
OFFER

Conceptual Model: **Why Do Boards Exist.**

Governance Solutions offers a world-class, **online director education program** where you can build competence and confidence in governance while you earn a ProDir® designation.

Whether you have a little or a lot of governance experience, this program will build the confidence, skills, knowledge, and competence in governance you need to make it in today's complex boardroom.

As a certified Professional Director®, you will enjoy the internationally recognized status as a graduate of one of the world's leading director education programs.

Start earning your ProDir® designation today with a free, introductory session—no obligation or credit card required. You'll instantly see the value and be one step closer to internationally recognized certification!

Start today at

ProfessionalDirector.com

BIBLIOGRAPHY

"About Us," Carbon Disclosure Project, accessed April 13, 2021, cdp.net/en/info/about-us.

"About Us," Safer Chemicals, Healthy Families, accessed April 14, 2021, saferchemicals.org/about/.

"Are You Wondering Is Tesla an ESG Stock?" Blogged Finance (blog), accessed April 5, 2021, bloggedfinance.com/tesla-esg-stock/.

"Canada Takes Action on the 2030 Agenda for Sustainable Development," Government of Canada, last modified February 17, 2021, canada. ca/en/employment-social-development/programs/ agenda-2030.html.

"ESG Ecosystem Map," World Economic Forum, 2019, widgets.weforum.org/esgecosystemmap/index.html#/ framework-developers/accountability-81.

"From Governance to Purpose to the Fundamental Reshaping of Finance: Analysis of Larry Fink's Annual Letter to CEOs," Globescan, January 22,

2020, globescan.com/analysis-larry-finksannual-letter-ceos-2020/.

"The Global Carbon Project," Global Carbon Project, accessed April 14, 2021, globalcarbonproject.org/.

"Global Reporting Initiative," World Economic Forum, accessed April 13, 2021, widgets.weforum.org/esgecosystemmap/index.html#/company/gri-5.

"Good Governance Driving Corporate Performance? A Meta-analysis of Academic Research and Invitation to Engage in the Dialogue," Deloitte, December 2016.

"Greenhouse Gas Protocol," World Economic Forum, accessed April 12, 2021, widgets.weforum.org/esgecosystemmap/index.html#/company/ghgprotocol-93.

"The GRI Standards: The Global Standards for Sustainability Reporting," GRI, accessed April 13, 2021, globalreporting.org/standards/media/2458/gri_standards_brochure.pdf.

"Leading by Example: Our Responsibility," World Economic Forum, accessed April 13, 2021, weforum.org/sustainability-world-economic-forum.

"MSCI Investor Relations," MSCI, accessed April 13, 2021, ir.msci.com/investor-relations?pagesect=AUM.

"Our Mission," World Economic Forum, accessed April 13, 2021, weforum.org/about/world-economic-forum.

"Our Planet," Amazon, accessed April 14, 2021, aboutamazon.com/planet.

"Report of the NACD Blue Ribbon Commission on Culture as a Corporate Asset," National Association of Corporate Directors, 2017.

"Subsidiaries of Metro," Retailer Report Card, accessed April 14, 2021, retailerreportcard.com/retailer/metro/.

"Subsidiaries of Restaurant Brands International," Retailer Report Card, accessed April 14, 2021, retailerreportcard.com/retailer/restaurant-brandsinternational/.

"Subsidiaries of Sobeys," Retailer Report Card, accessed April 14, 2021, retailerreportcard.com/retailer/sobeys/.

"Sustainability Review 2009," BP, accessed April 14, 2021, bp.com/content/dam/bp/business-sites/en/global/corporate/pdfs/sustainability/archive/archived-reports-and-translations/2009/bp_sustainability_review_2009.pdf.

"Sustainable Development Goals," United Nations, Department of Economic and Social Affairs, Sustainable Development, accessed April 13, 2021, sdgs.un.org/goals.

"Sustainalytics' ESG Risk Ratings Offer Clear Insight into the ESG Risks of Companies,"Sustainalytics, accessed April 13, 2021, sustainalytics.com/esgratings?currentpage=58.

"The 20 Critical Questions Series What Directors Should Ask About ESG,"The Institute of Internal Auditors, Australia, 2020, accessed April 14, 2021, iia.org.au/sf_docs/default-source/technical-resources/20-criticalquestions/20-questions-directors-should-ask-aboutesg.pdf?sfvrsn=2.

"Welcome to GRI," GRI, accessed April 23, 2021, globalreporting.org/.

"What We Do," CDP, accessed May 25, 2021, cdp.net/en/info/about-us/what-we-do.

"Who's Minding the Store?" Retailer Report Card, accessed April 14, 2021, retailerreportcard.com/.

"Wikipedia: Bhopal Disaster," Wikimedia Foundation, last edited May 30, 2021, 19:49, wikipedia.org/wiki/Bhopal.

"Wikipedia: Friedman Doctrine," Wikimedia Foundation, last edited May 7, 2021, 22:56, en.wikipedia.org/wiki/Friedman_doctrine.

"Wikipedia: Occupy Movement," Wikimedia Foundation, last edited June 5, 2021, 05:29, en.wikipedia.org/wiki/Occupy_movement.

"Wikipedia: Tsilqot'in Nation v British Columbia," Wikimedia Foundation, last edited May 27, 2021, 17:497, en.wikipedia.org/wiki/Tsilhqot%27in_Nation_v_British_Columbia.

Andrea Bonime-Blanc, "It's Time we Added a Letter to ESG. Here's Why," World Economic Forum,

October 14, 2020, weforum.org/agenda/2020/10/itstime-we-added-a-letter-to-esg-heres-why/.

Brown, David A. H. and Debra L. Brown. *Success in the Boardroom! 25 Years of Canadian Directorship Practices--1973-98*. Ottawa: Conference Board of Canada, 1998.

Brown, David, Debra L. Brown, and Vanessa Anastasopoulos. *Women on Boards: Not Just the Right Thing... but the "Bright" Thing*. Ottawa: Conference Board of Canada, 2002.

Brown, Dr. Debra L. and David A. H. Brown. *When Leaders Serve: Engaging the Board in Corporate Social*

Responsibility. Ottawa: The Conference Board of Canada, 1999.

Brown, Dr. Debra L. and David A. H. Brown. "When Leaders Serve: Engaging the Board in Corporate Social Responsibility," Ottawa: The Conference Board of Canada, 1999.

Committee on the Financial Aspects of Corporate Governance and Adrian Cadbury. *Report of the Committee on the Financial Aspects of Corporate Governance*. London: Gee, 1992.

The Greenhouse Gas Protocol: A Corporate Accounting and Reporting Standard, Greenhouse Gas Protocol, accessed April 13, 2021, ghgprotocol.org/ corporatestandard.

Franks, D.M., K. McNab, D. Brereton, T. Cohen, F. Weldegiorgis, T. Horberry, D. Lynas, M. Garcia-Vasquez, B.O. Santibáñez, R. Barnes, and B. McLellan, "Designing mining technology for social outcomes: Final Report of the Technology Futures Project," prepared for CSIRO Minerals Down Under Flagship, Minerals Futures Cluster Collaboration, by the Centre for Social Responsibility in Mining & the Minerals Industry Safety and Health Centre, Sustainable Minerals Institute, The University of Queensland, Brisbane, 2013.

Cameron French, "Tim Hortons, Metro Among Retailers in New Report's Toxic Chemicals 'Hall of Shame,'" CTV News, last updated Monday April 5, 2021 (5:06 p.m. EDT), ctvnews.ca/business/ tim-hortons-metro-among-retailers-in-new-reports-toxic-chemicals-hall-of-shame-1.5375158#. YG4c3mvmnmY.mailto.

Adam Hayes, "MSGI ESG Ratings," Investopedia, updated February 11, 2021, investopedia.com/msciesg-ratings-5111990.

Henisz, Witold, Tim Koller, and Robin Nuttall, "Five Ways That ESG Creates Value," McKinsey Quarterly, November 2019.

B. Khan, A. Nijhof, R. A. Diepeveen, & D. A. M. Melis, "Does Good Corporate Governance Lead to Better Firm Performance? Strategic Lessons from a Structured Literature Review," *Corporate Ownership & Control,* 15, no.4 (2018), 73-85, doi.org/10.22495/cocv15i4art7.

Kieren Moffat, Airong Zhang, "The Paths to Social Licence to Operate: An Integrative Model Explaining Community Acceptance of Mining," *Resources Policy,* no. 39 (2013), doi.org/10.1016/j.resourpol.2013.11.003.

R. Parsons, Justine Lacey, Kieren Moffat, "Maintaining Discursive Legitimacy of a Contested Practice: How the Australian Minerals Industry Understands its 'Social Licence to Operate,'" *Resources Policy,* no. 41 (2014), 83-90, doi.org/10.1016/j.resourpol.2014.04.002.

Professional Director Certification Program, professionaldirector.com/.

ENDNOTES

1   Witold Henisz, Tim Koller, and Robin Nuttall, "Five Ways That ESG Creates Value," *McKinsey Quarterly,* November 2019.

2   Adam Hayes, "MSGI ESG Ratings," *Investopedia,* updated February 11, 2021, investopedia.com/msci-esg-ratings-5111990.

3   "Are You Wondering Is Tesla an ESG Stock?" *Blogged Finance* (blog), accessed April 5, 2021, bloggedfinance.com/tesla-esg-stock.

4   "Are You Wondering Is Tesla an ESG Stock?" *Blogged Finance* (blog).

5   "Sustainability Review 2009," *BP,* accessed April 14, 2021, bp.com/content/dam/bp/business-sites/en/global/corporate/pdfs/sustainability/archive/archived-reports-and-translations/2009/bp_sustainability_review_2009.pdf.

6   "Wikipedia: Occupy Movement." Wikimedia
     Foundation, last edited June 5, 2021, 05:29,
     en.wikipedia.org/wiki/Occupy_movement.

7   "From Governance to Purpose to the Fundamental
     Reshaping of Finance: Analysis of Larry
     Fink's Annual Letter to CEOs," *Globescan,*
     published January 22, 2020, globescan.com/
     analysis-larry-finks-annual-letter-ceos-2020.

8   Dr. Debra L. Brown and David A. H. Brown, *When
     Leaders Serve: Engaging the Board in Corporate Social
     Responsibility* (Ottawa: The Conference Board of
     Canada, 1999).

9   *The internet of things* describes the networking of
     physical objects that takes place over the internet, for
     example, objects such as cars, appliances, thermostats,
     and other tangibles that are embedded with sensors,
     software, or other technologies that communicate
     using a connection to the internet.

10   Andrea Bonime-Blanc, "It's Time we Added a
     Letter to ESG. Here's Why," *World Economic Forum,*
     October 14, 2020, weforum.org/agenda/2020/10/
     its-time-we-added-a-letter-to-esg-heres-why.

11   "Our Mission," *World Economic Forum,*
     accessed April 13, 2021, weforum.org/about/
     world-economic-forum.

12   "Leading by Example: Our Responsibility," *World
     Economic Forum,* accessed April 13, 2021, weforum.
     org/sustainability-world-economic-forum.

13   "Leading by example: our responsibility," *World
     Economic Forum.*

14   "Our Planet," *Amazon,* accessed April 14, 2021.
     aboutamazon.com/planet.

15 "Our Planet," *Amazon.*

16 Cameron French, "Tim Hortons, Metro Among Retailers in New Report's Toxic Chemicals 'Hall of Shame,'" *CTV News,* last updated Monday April 5, 2021 (5:06 p.m. EDT), ctvnews.ca/business/tim-hortons-metro-among-retailers-in-new-reports-toxic-chemicals-hall-of-shame-1.5375158#.YG4c3mvmnmY.mailto.

17 "About Us," *Safer Chemicals, Healthy Families,* accessed April 14, 2021, saferchemicals.org/about.

18 "Who's Minding the Store?" *Retailer Report Card,* accessed April 14, 2021, retailerreportcard.com.

19 "Subsidiaries of Metro," *Retailer Report Card,* accessed April 14, 2021. retailerreportcard.com/retailer/metro.

20 "Subsidiaries of Sobeys," *Retailer Report Card,* accessed April 14, 2021, retailerreportcard.com/retailer/sobeys.

21 "Subsidiaries of Restaurant Brands International," *Retailer Report Card,* accessed April 14, 2021, retailerreportcard.com/retailer/restaurant-brands-international.

22 "Subsidiaries of Restaurant Brands International," *Retailer Report Card.*

23 "What We Do," *CDP,* accessed May 25, 2021, cdp.net/en/info/about-us/what-we-do.

24 "Welcome to GRI," *GRI,* accessed April 23, 2021, globalreporting.org.

25 "The GRI Standards: The Global Standards for Sustainability Reporting," *GRI,* accessed April 13, 2021, globalreporting.org/standards/media/2458/gri_standards_brochure.pdf.

26   "The GRI Standards: The Global Standards for Sustainability Reporting," *GRI.*

27   "Global Reporting Initiative," *World Economic Forum,* accessed April 13, 2021, widgets.weforum.org/ esgecosystemmap/index.html#/company/gri-5.

28   "ESG Ecosystem Map," *World Economic Forum,* 2019, widgets.weforum.org/esgecosystemmap/index.html#/ framework-developers/accountability-81.

29   *The Greenhouse Gas Protocol: A Corporate Accounting and Reporting Standard,* Greenhouse Gas Protocol, accessed April 13, 2021, ghgprotocol.org/ corporate-standard.

30   "Greenhouse Gas Protocol," *World Economic Forum,* accessed April 12, 2021, widgets.weforum. org/esgecosystemmap/index.html#/company/ ghg-protocol-93.

31   "Sustainable Development Goals," *United Nations, Department of Economic and Social Affairs, Sustainable Development,* accessed April 13, 2021, sdgs.un.org/ goals.

32   "Canada Takes Action on the 2030 Agenda for Sustainable Development," *Government of Canada,* last modified February 17, 2021, canada.ca/en/ employment-social-development/programs/ agenda-2030.html.

33   "Sustainable Development Goals," *United Nations, Department of Economic and Social Affairs, Sustainable Development.*

34   "The Global Carbon Project." *Global Carbon Project,* accessed April 14, 2021, globalcarbonproject.org.

35   "About Us," *Carbon Disclosure Project,* accessed April 13, 2021, cdp.net/en/info/about-us.

36 "MSCI Investor Relations," *MSCI,* accessed April 13, 2021, ir.msci.com/investor-relations?pagesect=AUM.

37 "Sustainalytics' ESG Risk Ratings Offer Clear Insight into the ESG Risks of Companies," *Sustainalytics,* accessed April 13, 2021 sustainalytics. com/esg-ratings?currentpage=58.

38 D.M. Franks, K. McNab, D. Brereton, T. Cohen, F. Weldegiorgis, T. Horberry, D. Lynas, M. Garcia-Vasquez, B.O. Santibáñez, R. Barnes, and B. McLellan, "Designing mining technology for social outcomes: Final Report of the Technology Futures Project." Prepared for CSIRO Minerals Down Under Flagship, Minerals Futures Cluster Collaboration, by the Centre for Social Responsibility in Mining & the Minerals Industry Safety and Health Centre, Sustainable Minerals Institute, The University of Queensland, Brisbane, 2013.

39 R. Parsons, Justine Lacey, Kieren Moffat, "Maintaining Discursive Legitimacy of a Contested Practice: How the Australian Minerals Industry Understands its 'Social Licence to Operate,'" *Resources Policy,* no. 41 (2014), 83-90 doi. org/10.1016/j.resourpol.2014.04.002.

40 Kieren, Moffat, Airong Zhang, "The Paths to Social Licence to Operate: An Integrative Model Explaining Community Acceptance of Mining," *Resources Policy,* no. 39 (2013), doi.org/10.1016/j. resourpol.2013.11.003.

41 "Wikipedia: Bhopal Disaster," Wikimedia Foundation, last edited May 30, 2021, 19:49, wikipedia.org/wiki/Bhopal.

42   "Wikipedia: *Tsilqot'in Nation v British Columbia,*" Wikimedia Foundation, last edited May 27, 2021, 17:497, en.wikipedia.org/wiki/Tsilhqot%27in_Nation_v_British_Columbia.

43   "Wikipedia: Friedman Doctrine." Wikimedia Foundation, last edited May 7, 2021, 22:56, en.wikipedia.org/wiki/Friedman_doctrine.

44   David A.H. Brown, and Debra L. Brown, *Success in the Boardroom! 25 Years of Canadian Directorship Practices--1973-98* (Ottawa: Conference Board of Canada, 1998).

45   "Good Governance Driving Corporate Performance? A Meta-analysis of Academic Research and Invitation to Engage in the Dialogue," *Deloitte,* December 2016.

46   B. Khan, A. Nijhof, R. A. Diepeveen, & D. A. M. Melis, "Does Good Corporate Governance Lead to Better Firm Performance? Strategic Lessons from a Structured Literature Review," *Corporate Ownership & Control,* 15, no.4 (2018), 73-85, doi.org/10.22495/cocv15i4art7.

47   Committee on the Financial Aspects of Corporate Governance and Adrian Cadbury, *Report of the Committee on the Financial Aspects of Corporate Governance* (London: Gee, 1992).

48   "The 20 Critical Questions Series What Directors Should Ask About ESG," *The Institute of Internal Auditors,* Australia, 2020, accessed April 14, 2021, iia.org.au/sf_docs/default-source/technical-resources/20-critical-questions/20-questions-directors-should-ask-about-esg.pdf?sfvrsn=2.

49 David Brown, Debra L. Brown, and Vanessa Anastasopoulos, *Women on Boards: Not Just the Right Thing... but the "Bright" Thing* (Ottawa, ON: Conference Board of Canada, 2002).

50 "Report of the NACD Blue Ribbon Commission on Culture as a Corporate Asset," *National Association of Corporate Directors*, 2017.

51 Access the "Boardroom Culture Solution©" assessment tool here: governancesolutions.ca/store?viewType=productView&productId=21. Use the code TRYME to obtain your free access.

52 Access the "Top Ten Markers of a High Performance Board" self assessment tool here: governancesolutions.ca/governance-solutions/publications/highperformancemarkersboard.

53 "What We Do," *Balanced Scorecard West Africa,* accessed June 12, 2021, balancedscorecardwa.org/what-we-do/.

54 Professional Director Certification Program, professionaldirector.com.

Manufactured by Amazon.ca
Bolton, ON